A LONDON
COUNTRY
DIARY

Mundane Happenings from the
Secret Streets of the Capital

Tim Bradford

Published in the UK in 2014 by
Icon Books Ltd, Omnibus Business Centre,
39–41 North Road, London N7 9DP
email: info@iconbooks.net
www.iconbooks.net

Sold in the UK, Europe and Asia
by Faber & Faber Ltd, Bloomsbury House,
74–77 Great Russell Street,
London WC1B 3DA or their agents

Distributed in the UK, Europe and Asia
by TBS Ltd, TBS Distribution Centre, Colchester Road,
Frating Green, Colchester CO7 7DW

Distributed in Australia and New Zealand
by Allen & Unwin Pty Ltd,
PO Box 8500, 83 Alexander Street,
Crows Nest, NSW 2065

Distributed in South Africa by
Jonathan Ball, Office B4, The District,
41 Sir Lowry Road, Woodstock 7925

Distributed in India by Penguin Books India,
11 Community Centre, Panchsheel Park,
New Delhi 110017

Distributed in Canada by
Penguin Books Canada,
90 Eglinton Avenue East, Suite 700,
Toronto, Ontario M4P 2YE

Published in the USA by Icon Books Ltd,
39–41 North Road, London N7 9DP, UK
Distributed to the trade in the USA by
Consortium Book Sales and Distribution,
The Keg House, 34 Thirteenth Avenue NE,
Suite 101, Minneapolis, Minnesota 55413-1007

ISBN: 978-184831-705-5

Design by Doug Cheeseman

Printed and bound in the UK by Clays Ltd, St Ives plc

To You...

You talked to the magic trees.
You helped me fight off the giant pirates.
You loved the football tree.

You stood in the leaves with me.
You said we should be Vikings.
You found a beautiful stone.

You danced on the big tree stump.
You persuaded me to buy hot chocolate in the park.
You saw how it was all connected.

You lay on the grass and stared at the clouds
You walked with me in the wild wind.
You showed me new paths.

A SERIES OF
NON-ADVENTURES

This rambling and ramshackle diary reflects my
need to go wandering, and my attempts to reconcile
a need to appreciate and record nature with my
love of urban life. As a child in the wilds of rural
Lincolnshire I would rarely have to stray more than
a mile from the lanes and fields near our house and,
thirty years on, I still keep a small orbit – Highbury
Corner to the south, Seven Sisters Road/Finsbury
Park to the north, Stoke Newington High Street to
the east and Holloway Road to the west. Imagine the
Hundred Acre Wood populated by drunk football
fans, abandoned cars, old pubs, quiet cafes, TVs with
kids' programmes, mums with prams and strange
little run-down parks.

The seemingly random entries date from the end
of the 90s through to 2014, and in a subtle way chart
my steady progress from starry-eyed urban explorer
with a desire to articulate the Zen wondrousness of
city life to slightly hassled dad trying to catch buses/
trying to get the kids to school on time/trying not to
burn fish fingers (yet still finding time to walk about/
stare out of the window and gawp at stuff).

The common thread is (I hope) my belief in
the beauty of the mundane, my love of saluting to
magpies, wondering about the trees, drawing plants
I don't know the name of, trying to imagine the

past, attempting to befriend mice, watching blossom blowing at the side of the road, trying not to listen to foxes having sex in our back garden, talking to old people, watching buses, breaking up fights, looking at heavy machinery with the kids and my faith in the unifying properties of old urban pubs. All of life is here in these pages.

Actually, it isn't. It's just a really tiny slice of life, the non-news that just-about-happens within a square mile of my house.

Tim Bradford, 2014
(on a 19 bus that's stuck in traffic)

INTRODUCTION

by Stewart Lee

Like some hardy weed clinging to a hostile cliff face, Tim Bradford is himself a survivor. A freelance writer and illustrator, he holds his ground in a North London enclave, until a decade or so ago the natural habitat for him and his kind, but now colonised by hedge-fund managers and business types, cropping the marsh grass upon which he once fed so peacefully, and whereupon he took his ease. Bradford's ilk are now largely gone from their ancestral homelands, to Brighton, Bristol, Whitstable, and Walthamstow. But Bradford has survived and adapted, like the pubs that spit out their old regulars in search of the gastro dollar, or the unreconstructed working men's clubs further east, now doubling up as ironic burlesque venues for moustachioed Shoreditch hipsters. And Bradford's latest work, *A London Country Diary*, is the literary equivalent of this adaptation.

A London Country Diary quietly appropriates the style and presentation of its rural country diary forebears, among them Edith Blackwell Holden's posthumously published 1906 opus, *The Country Diary of An Edwardian Lady*, Robert Gibbings' once best-selling river books of the 40s, and Alison Uttley's several volumes of recollections of her late 19th century Derbyshire countryside childhood. Like these earlier titles, Bradford's cornucopia of unrelated observations flits gadfly-like between various subjects and scenes, but all are to be found in the highways and byways of Stoke Newington, Hackney and Highbury, rather than in the fields and waterways of a forgotten and romanticised rural England.

Nonetheless, in the clatter of the Arsenal Cafe, the abandoned bowling green of Clissold Park, the lost New River Milestone, the scavenging foxes of Riversdale Road, and the snails of his own back garden, Bradford begins to apprehend an absurd vision of The Sublime, as surely as his landscape-loving literary forebears Edward Thomas and Ithell Colquhoun saw their own apparitions of The Great God Pan along *The Icknield Way*, or in the *The Living Stones* of Ireland and Cornwall, respectively.

Even *A London Country Diary*'s illustrations seem to echo the presentation of these earlier works. C.F. Tunnicliffe's vivid etchings illuminate Uttley's recollections. The polymath Gibbings' own graceful lines wend through his river diaries. Colquhoun reins in her surrealist tendencies to illustrate her travel books. Bradford describes his own artworks as 'wang-eyed pop art', but contextualised within the country diary format, they seem, in their own wang-eyed way, to be firmly in the illustrative tradition of Tunnicliffe or Gibbings or Denys Watkins-Pitchford; flashing in on random details, skewing our perception of the text. And while Bradford's occasional maps are not strictly geographically accurate, in the way Alfred Wainwright's pen and ink cartographies of the Lakeland Fells undeniably were, they nonetheless have form and function. I fell into step alongside Bradford early one morning off Blackstock Road to find we were both heading west into town on foot – but his route was that of a rat, steeped in the swiftest routes, not that of some opportunistic sat nav jockey trying his idle hand at minicabbing.

Bradford is not alone in the idea that chance encounters with apparently meaningless phenomena may, if persisted with, provoke some mild form of enlightenment. Arthur Machen (1863-1947) was perhaps the progenitor of Bradford's breed of mystic-flâneurs. The detailed descriptions of apparently aimless wandering in his 1924 shambles, *The London Adventure*, quietly approach the profound. In Machen's wake, also foreshadowing Bradford, we find Frank Baker's 1948 travelogue, *The Road Is Free*, detailing the varied characters and places encountered during a road trip the length of Britain under rationing, that almost seems to be a plea for a new society.

But it is Iain Sinclair who is the post-Velvet Underground Glam Rock Lou Reed to Tim Bradford's Glam Pop Alvin Stardust. Sinclair's more obviously experimental poetry and prose of the 70s has latterly been supplanted by more immediately accessible, but no less vital, essays, polemics and playful prose exercises, in the character of an often unreliable narrator, all disguised as apparently unplanned outgrowths from superficially idle urban rambles, many of them through the same postcodes Bradford himself traverses. But where Sinclair sees the city pavements scarred by the claws of global capitalism, corporate greed, and the ongoing annihilation of the individual, Bradford sees simply weeds, slugs, and foxes tugging at an abandoned pizza, and leaves us to make of these symbols whatever we will, their meaning resolutely un-glossed, and only barely implied.

Is Bradford himself in *A London Country Diary*, or is the Bradford we read about in the book a simplified and satirically useful version of himself, as in the cartoon Bradford that occasionally appears on his website? The Czech surrealist Carel Capek's 1925 travelogue *Letters From England* sees the author cast himself as a bewildered innocent abroad, so as best to ridicule our country, slipping into a tradition solidified by the wide-eyed heroes of earlier, albeit fictional, accounts of travellers at odds with unfathomable cultures. Like Raphael as far back as 1516 in Thomas More's *Utopia*, Swift's eponymous Lemuel Gulliver of 1716, or Arthur Dent in *The Hitchhiker's Guide to the Galaxy*, is Bradford his own self-operated observer-character, a giant beside a Subbuteo figure, a dwarf before the cultural chasm left when Stoke Newington's Vortex Jazz Club was replaced by a Nando's?

And is the North London Bradford portrays in *A London Country Diary* even real? I recognise it, vividly, but various readers of Francis Brett Young's 1937 description of day-to-day life in Worcestershire village of Monk's Norton, *Portrait of a Village*, beautifully illustrated by Joan Hassall's line drawings, wrote to him to say how accurately it reflected their own memories of the place, despite the fact that Young had completely fabricated the village and all its inhabitants, in part as a parody of this whole strain of country diary literature. Is Bradford assembling a quasi-fictional world on top of a less satisfying real one, by allowing himself to focus in on fascinating details at the expense of the dispiriting reality?

I suspect *A London Country Diary* may have political and philosophical dimensions, though I am not sure if Bradford is aware of them, and have no intention of asking him. It is not his job to explain. The progress from W.H. Hudson's 1887 utopian science fiction novel, *A Crystal Age*, to his romanticised 1910 account of the lives of rural workers on the Wiltshire Downs, *A Shepherd's Life*, is all too obvious. Both are politically prescriptive, but the latter used actual observations of the natural world to kick-start a back to the land movement that sucked in a generation of literary types, including Ronald Duncan, whose 1964 memoir of his pre-war bolt for a better life in North Devon, *All Men Are Islands*, might be another progenitor of *A London Country Diary*.

None of us can help but look for our own reflection in whatever art we stumble across. I stand at the precipice Bradford has already negotiated,

the 'should I stay or should I go?' dilemma faced by
anyone who came to London as a twenty-something
to chase their dreams, and now finds it increasingly
unwelcoming, inappropriate to their adult needs.
The forests and fields of cultural memory beckon
us, whether we actually experienced them in
infancy or not, and yet the global population is
increasingly urbanised. The lexicon of poetry, of art,
of literature, was historically composed of natural
images, but who do the woodland flora and fauna
of Thomas Hardy, Edward Thomas, and even Ted
Hughes speak to now? In supplanting the country
diary format of old, however lightheartedly, with
his own ramshackle version, Bradford seems to be
suggesting that, denied the instant contact high of
field and stream, we seek instead our communion
with the sublime in the minutiae of city living. His
latest book is either the end of an old tradition, or
the start of a new one.

I own one of Bradford's 'wang-eyed' paintings. I
didn't know him well when I bought it. His wife had
complained that their home was full of his unsold
art, so he organised a fire sale at a local library. 'The
Lost Dolmen of Cahermachrusheen' depicts a stone
farm wall, presumably assembled from the wreckage
of a missing-presumed-demolished prehistoric
burial chamber, once recorded as standing nearby,
in the barren Burren of North Clare in the West
of Ireland. Bradford depicts the original dolmen,
shimmering in the bottom left of the canvas like

a Scooby-Doo ghost, a helpful arrow indicating
its presumed transformation into the functional
containing wall.

My own second-hand copy of W.H. Hudson's *The
Book of a Naturalist* (a 1919 manifestation of the country
diary trope complete with chapter titles like 'Hints To
Adder Seekers', 'The Toad As Traveller', 'Concerning
Lawns and Earthworms' and 'A Friendly Rat') has
pressed leaves of trees placed between the pages by
the original owner. It is sobering to note that it
is statistically likely that at least one of the species
preserved is no longer native to the British Isles, or
is in imminent danger of disappearance. Bradford
accepts that our increased urbanisation, and the
demonstrable incremental reduction in the sheer
abundance of visible nature around us, renders the
country diary literature of old a distant prospect. But
he unsentimentally embraces its approach in order to
deal with his own urban experience, the ghost of the
template he has assimilated still flickering beneath
the surface.

Arthur Machen's 1935 novella, *N*, imagines
then suburban Stoke Newington as a gateway to a
hidden world, occasionally glimpsed, that exists in
tandem with the streets and parks of N16, overlaid
like a tracing paper map. Bradford shows us that the
doorway to that alternative world is always open, if we
stare long enough at leaves trapped in ice, Victorian
gas holders, and faded photos in a chemist's window.

Stewart Lee, writer/clown

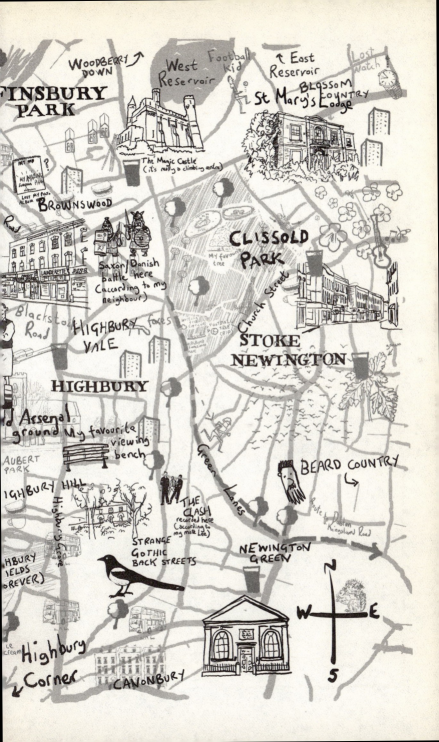

WINTER
(well, sort of late winter)

BLACKSTOCK ROAD

If the definition of a perfect street is somewhere with plentiful dry cleaners, launderettes, old men's pubs, Chinese takeaways, hardware shops, fruit and veg stalls, cafes and somewhere to buy a hamster, then Blackstock Road is almost perfect (the hamster emporium closed a few years ago).

THE ARSENAL CAFE, BLACKSTOCK ROAD

There are so many with virtually the same name around here. Anyway, they do a great bacon and tomato sandwich on thick crusty white. Free *Daily Mirror* to read while you're waiting.

The owner looks like the actor Paul Sorvino.

FOX RODENT
HYBRID NUT FIENDS

A mother is walking through the park with a small boy following behind, dribbling a football. A squirrel runs across their path.

'I used to see red squirrels when I was little,' says Mum. The boy isn't listening. He's doing commentaries to himself as he jogs along.

'There were lots of them at my Auntie Jo's house,' she says. The boy kicks the ball against the fence and makes a crowd noise. His mum sighs.

'They're mostly grey squirrels now.'

THE 2008 TWO-PAGES-PER-DAY DESK DIARY

The 2008 two-pages-per-day desk diary is the biggest diary I have ever bought. The bloke at the stationers' shop asked if I was going to be writing out every single thing that happened during the day in order to fill up the two pages of A4, 'You know, like "got up in the morning", that kind of thing.' It made me think that the 2008 two-pages-per-day desk diary was only on sale in his shop to ensnare passing anal-retentives for the purposes of mockery.

I intend to start doing arm curls of the 2008 two-pages-per-day desk diary. Then when I enter the World Stationery Lifting Championships my local stationer will be laughing on the other side of his face.

HOW TO GET A PLASTIC BOOMERANG BACK FROM YOUR NEXT DOOR NEIGHBOUR

My kids got a yellow plastic boomerang thing a few weeks ago. I attempted to show them how it worked. It sailed over the fence into next door's garden but didn't sail back.

An hour or so later I saw our neighbour and said, 'Our yellow plastic boomerang thing is in your garden. Can you chuck it back for us?'

'Yeah, sure,' he said.

'The yellow plastic boomerang thing will soon be back,' I said to the kids. But it didn't come back. For several days it stayed in the same place in their garden. Next time I saw our neighbour I kind of did boomerang actions with my hands. Possibly my attempt at mime looked like I was saying he was a wanker because our neighbour resolutely ignored the boomerang thing for another week. He even walked about in his garden and probably trod on the yellow plastic boomerang thing.

I didn't see him for ages after that. He was avoiding me. Perhaps he'd tried throwing it back but it kept returning to his garden. Then, just before Christmas, the boomerang thing returned. What a great guy our next door neighbour is.

As soon as it gets a bit warmer I shall be showing my kids how to use it.

FLAME STOOL

Under a young tree on the pavement lies a charred pile of stuff – pieces of clothing, books, aerosol cans and a small stool. A pair of men's shoes are still slightly smouldering, the aftermath, no doubt, of some apocalyptic relationship breakup. Or perhaps a young graffiti-addicted accountant simply spontaneously combusted on his stargazing stool while contemplating the sheer joy of life.

Lost →

MR RABBIT,
CAUGHT IN THE RAIN

The rains are sheeting down on a midwinter
afternoon. As I walk through the eastern section
of the park I notice a limp form draped over the
fence. As I get closer I see it is a child's rabbit teddy,
soaked through, with one eye missing and am hit
by a wave of strange sad nostalgia for my days of
galumphing around here with prams and kids-on-
shoulders. How has it all gone so quickly? I pick up
the teddy and it lies soaking and limp in my hand.
For a moment I am paralysed by indecision. What
to do? There is nothing I can do. Best to leave it
here in case they come back to look for it. Like those
photojournalists who snap pics in stressful wartime
conditions, I do a sketch of Mr Bunbun then leave
him to his fate. I feel bad, but I put it back and carry
on walking through the rain.

ALED UP

The sound of Aled Jones singing fills the streets of Highbury Vale. Perhaps a fan of squeaky chorister recordings has moved in to the area. Or it's the Welsh songbird himself (possibly showing off to a new girlfriend in his bedsit). Either way, it's bad news.

SHEDS

- **SENSIBLE**
- **HOMELY**
- **ECO FRIENDLY (sometimes)**
- **DREARY**

Want to escape from your family into the wonderful world of paint, nails, tools and plastic toys that need to go to the recycling centre? Then you need a shed.

Sheds came to Britain with the Romans. Before that, people kept their gardening equipment in holes in the ground.

At the International Shed Corporation, we have sheds of all shapes and sizes to meet your needs. Though mostly we've just got flatpacked little sheds with one window and really crap instructions.

The International Shed Corporation

SEE SHED SHE SAID

My wife sent me an email about sheds. I knew, instinctively, that something had subtly shifted in my experience of life. That I was heading down a new road. Like most relationships, there had been a time when we used to send each other daily love letters, excited plans for beer sessions or just little poems. Now, all of a sudden, it was sheds. I accepted with a sigh the onward passage of time and replied in some sort of trying-to-be-funny-are-you-sure-you-meant-to-send-this-to-me-and-not-your-dad kind of way, but she relentlessly followed it up with more emails containing pictures of sheds. At first I tried to rebuff her shed offensive with more off-the-cuff humour. Then I emailed back and said that we already had a shed. It didn't work.

'That's not a shed,' she said, 'it's an outsized wooden box with a lid that keeps falling down on top of your head. Do you want to get permanent brain damage every time you do a bit of gardening?' I was outgunned. Eventually I had to admit defeat and enter the world of sheds, where my wife had already taken up residence and set herself up as Queen.

BEAUTIFUL LILY PETALS

Walking down our street towards the house I notice some beautiful white lily petals on the pavement in front of a neighbour's house. But how did they get there? It's too early for lilies . . . and where are the plants? No matter, lily petals are always lovely and uplifting.

In folk medicine lily petals have been used for removing calluses, warts, boils, bruises, pimples and earache. Possibly someone nearby is growing a medieval herb/medicine garden.

It's only as I get closer that I realise they are actually discarded prawn crackers. Next to them lies a pile of mouldy-looking fried rice.

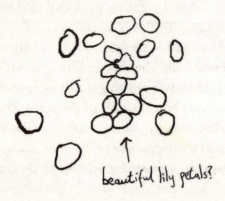

beautiful lily petals?

CLISSOLD PARK BOWLING
GREEN MARTIAL ARTS SOCIETY

The old bowling green in Clissold Park has recently
become a martial arts zone. Of particular interest
is the modern hybrid form practised by two white-
tracksuited youngsters. It looks to be a combination
of tai chi, judo, robotic dancing and generally
hanging around looking bored. Quite how this form
would fare in straight combat is hard to say, though
the bright white robes/shellsuits might be off-putting
enough to an attacker for the martial artists to leg it
in the other direction.

found in pocket

SHOW AND TELL DAY

It was Show and Tell Day today in year one but my
six-year-old was in tears, having forgotten to bring
in anything again. Luckily I have jeans full of 'stuff'
– today I found a small antique compass deep in one
of my pockets and told him it had once belonged
to Captain Jack Sparrow. He seemed placated and
began to piece together his story of how he came to
have it, which involved rockpools and quite a few
mermaids.

I think they will have to rebrand it as Show and Lie
Day.

HIGHGATE WOOD

This magical area is one of the few remaining parcels of the ancient Forest of Middlesex. It's great to disappear into these shape-shifting woods for an hour or two and escape from the reality of urban life. Sometimes I have to try hard to stop my spirit floating away off to Highgate Wood . . .

COLLAPSING OLD BUILDINGS

The little print shop next to The Gunners pub has
collapsed. For several days workmen* had been
gutting the building and digging down into its
foundations, presumably in a madcap attempt to
burrow into the public bar of The Gunners and steal
some valuable signed photos of 1971 Double-winning
skipper Frank McClintock. Blackstock Road was
closed for a couple of days so the buses had to come
down our road. On Monday morning, as I tried to
confront the usual nappy shit, Weetabix globules and
The Tweenies at full volume, some people looked
down into our sitting room from the no. 19 bus and
collectively let out a sigh of relief that they weren't
me.

* I use this term loosely – it was actually just a few blokes with digging
equipment which they were obviously using for the first time.

green
patterned
dress

leggings
↓

PUBLISHING
GIRL

**Woman I Saw Walk Into a Publisher's in West
London a Few Years Ago (Might Have Been an
Interesting Poet. Or Perhaps the CEO.)**

DRESSED FOR THE H-BOMB

A grey day, too miserable to play in the park but perfect weather for a walk north along Blackstock Road to the rather snazzy Finsbury Park Library. The kids snaffle up a range of books, Jacqueline Wilson, *Star Wars*, *Biff and Chip*, annuals, but I am drawn to the CD section and while browsing absentmindedly I am suddenly face to face with a gem, the *Rough Trade – Post Punk Volume 1* double CD. To be honest I felt it was worth the 50p just to hear the first track, 'I Found That Essence Rare', by Gang of Four for the first time in ages. It sounded so funky, edgy and excitable that I had to laugh.

Gang of Four's first album, *Entertainment*, was genius. I think people at the time (and by that I mean every single adult in Britain in 1979) were split into two camps – the Joy Division introverted bedroom moroseness 'I can't get girls' blokes, and the Gang of Four loudmouth banging on about politics and feminism 'I can't get girls' blokes (of which I was one).

After I'd listened to it for about the sixth time a wave of melancholy swept over me when I realised that it's from around 30 years ago. Those beautiful lasses from Delta 5 are probably grannies now. Plus I had already incurred a fine for not getting the CD back to the library in time.

SPRING

(could start anywhere
between January and April)

CLISSOLD PARK

London's most beautiful park, and over the years home to all kinds of magic trees, giant pirates, evil witches, football matches, rugby matches, teddy bears' picnics, summer beer sessions, and where everyone learns to ride a bike. Also contains a nice ornamental stretch of what remains of the New River, a watercourse built in the early 1600s to bring drinking water from Hertfordshire to the City of London (puffs on an invisible pipe . . .).

IS THIS SPRING?

Yesterday I saw the first ladybird of spring. It landed on the screen of my Mac while I was checking the latest Premiership table. Then the phone rang. It was a woman from the Alliance and Leicester asking if I'd like a loan. They're pissed off with me because I recently paid off the balance on my credit card and are trying strong-arm tactics to get me back on the high interest bandwagon. After I'd told her to get lost I went back to play with my new insect friend. But the ladybird had gone.

It rained all day today. Various little streams have appeared in the roads, all pouring down the Hackney Brook valley at different points. The two biggest run down Green Lanes and diagonally north-east through Clissold Park towards Grazebrook Road. I was splashing about in one of them when a car horn hooted and a woman leaned out of the window, fag in mouth, looking at me. I walked over to the car.

- Are you lost?
- What?
- What?

Then she stared past me, up at the block of flats across the road, and blew smoke on my waterproof.

35

THE ORIGINS OF DANEBOTTOM

My six-year-old son often asks me, when we walk up Canning Road, to tell him about the Viking battle of Blackstock Road.

'How do you know about that?' I said the other day.

'You told me.'

OK. I did read something about that when I was writing my previous book about underground rivers, and must have mentioned it to him once. So I took to researching — on the internet, you understand — where the story originally comes from.

The oldest source of the story is the archived paper 'Perambulations in Islington' by Thomas Edlyne Tomlins (1858). In this he mentions Danebottom several times, for example:'some battle fought there in earlier times, perhaps so far back as the period of the Danish incursions, the memory of which, as I have ventured to suggest, has been traditionally preserved in Danebottom, at Highbury Vale.' In fact, Blackstock Road had apparently been known as Danebottom Lane for many centuries.

There is no older source for this story but what Tomlins is saying, essentially, is that the Saxons held the bridge over the Hackney Brook, presumably near the Arsenal Tavern, and the Danes came down from the heights of Finsbury Park and tried to 'take' the Arsenal Tavern, er, I mean bridge.

It would be great if there was some kind of North London version of York's Jorvik Viking Centre erected on Blackstock Road — maybe in one of the vacant small shops on the street.

POSH BLOKE
GOES TO DUBLIN

The tall posh bloke from down the road went to Dublin last weekend to 'watch the rugger'. He had a 'damn good time' (he told his mate in the local newsagents) and 'can't really remember much about it'. His mate, a South African, said, 'Wow, min! Did yi sii thi Wils Frinss gim is will?'

ON THE FENCE

Walking through Clissold Park this morning,
pushing the pram, I noticed one of the deer had
its antlers caught in the wire fence. The more it
struggled to break free the more it got tangled up. I
got a passing cyclist to give me a leg-up then scaled
the 10-foot-high fence and prepared to drop down
the other side. Suddenly the deer freed itself and I
was left hanging, no longer an animal welfare have-
a-go-hero but all of a sudden a trespasser likely to
incur a Hackney Council fine. I managed to flip
myself back over and luckily my fall was broken
by the cyclist who was still anxiously watching my
progress. He picked himself up, gave me a weak smile
(obviously thinking 'inept tosser') and pedalled off.
I collected the pram and my son and strode off to
the north.

HACKNEY BROOK
AND BAYERN MUNICH

Coinciding with a massive hangover on my part caused by an impossible-to-turn-down lock-in the night before, the Hackney Brook (the old stream that used to run west-east across Blackstock Road before being culverted in the 19th century) appears to have resurfaced on Blackstock Road, just south of the Arsenal Tavern. Not caused by heavy rains this time, but by a large yellow JCB, which has dug a huge hole in the side of the road. Water shoots out of a pipe and into what's becoming a quite decent sized pond. My young son is very impressed. 'Digger!' 'River!' He dances up and down on the pavement. We go to the Gunners' Fish Bar for lunch, where we meet a group of Bayern Munich fans in town for tonight's Champions League game. They have come for some hot Pukka Pies. Blackstock Road is certainly at its most beautiful for these visitors – shit weather, grey skies, soggy chips. And huge puddles in the road.

I notice that one of the Germans looks like Nigel Winterburn and mention it to my little boy. For some reason he is not impressed.

'LUSCIOUS RENDEZVOUS'

I'm really excited to see that there's a cafe on Blackstock Road called 'Luscious Rendezvous'. Think it must be a rebranding. Was it 'Dave's Kebabs' before?

THE MAGIC CASTLE
(it's really a climbing centre)

not magic

not magic

magic

not magic

THE MAGIC CASTLE
AND THE MAGIC TREES

When my daughter was a very little girl we would walk through Clissold Park every day, and she would point into the distance at castellated turrets above the trees and shout, 'A magic castle! Daddy, is that a magic castle?' And, being a believer in truth and plain speaking, I would look at the rock climbing centre and reply, 'Yes, love, it is a magic castle. Course it is.' And then, embarrassed by this, I would change the subject to something more prosaic, such as, 'Oh no, here come the evil witches from behind the bowling green. Let's run!' And I'd push her pushchair really fast down the slope and she'd squeal with delight.

Not many locals know this, but in those days Clissold Park also had magic trees, which talked in Yorkshire accents and had little chocolates growing on the end of their branches (strangely similar to those tiny choccy stars that they sell in the newsagent's on Church Street). The other trees were mean and posh and didn't have free goodies for little kids.

The first time my daughter went to a party at the local climbing centre/pirate playhouse at the old late-Victorian London Water Board pumping station (the reality of the magic castle) she was slightly confused.

'Dad?'

'Evil witches! Run!'

FEUD CRITICS

The gambler who lives at the end of the road has
got himself into a feud with the frowning old man
who lives in a house opposite. Something to do with
keeping his lights on at night. Frowning old man says
it's anti-social then seems to suggest that if we'd all
followed Enoch Powell's advice none of these sorts of
issues would arise. The gambler – not usually lost for
words – finds it hard to argue with this line of attack.
Where do you begin? Instead, as I pass, he points to
his shoes, which are new, and asks if I like them. The
frowning old man frowns again.

THE BLUE PHOTOS

At the chemist on Green Lanes there are some beautiful, slightly blue-tinged photos in the window for people to look at and smile. Somehow these dog-eared photos in the window are some of the best in the whole of North London. These CIBA-chrome cardboard cut-outs are now wonderfully faded and sad-looking. They must have been put there during the classic late 70s/early 80s period by a design-minded pharmacist (or pharmacist's assistant).

The subliminal message of the blue photos is, of course, 'And while you're staring at them, why not come in the shop and buy some toothpaste. We've got loads!'

SPRING ON THE 19 BUS ROUTE

An Upper Street walk.
Drinkers stand near the bus stop.
Wi-Fi workers stare.

Cherry blossom floats
through the air like soft pink snow
near the council offices.

THE PHILOSOPHY OF FROGS

I came across another possible solution to my snail problem one night while out drinking with Billy, a gardener friend. After the pub had kicked us out we piled back to Billy's house. As we got to his front door, Billy (a big chap) boomed, 'Some fucker has stolen my fucking plum tree!' He inspected the traces of soil where the pot had been, then smiled. 'Fancy a whiskey?' Over a Jameson's or two he showed me his tadpole collection in a tank in the kitchen. I decided that getting some frogs would be the 'old woman who swallowed a fly' way of dealing with garden pests such as snails and slugs.

No problem, said Billy. He poured another whiskey then gave me a selection of tadpoles in a tupperware container. An hour or so later I staggered home with my tadpoles, pissed as a newt and feeling like a boy who'd just won a goldfish at the fair. I put them in the small pond I'd made the year before from the goose feeder my father-in-law had ordered during his phase of being a west of Ireland goose farmer. If the frogs did too well, at some point I'd

 need birds to get rid of them. Then a cat to get rid of the birds, a dog to get rid of the cat and possibly a crocodile to get rid of the dog. And then an armoured car to get rid of the crocodile.

No. 19 Bus

NEVER LET HER SLIP AWAY

This morning I was sitting on the top deck of a
no. 19 bus. Around Highbury Corner the conductor
started to whistle the tune to Andrew Gold's 'Never
Let Her Slip Away'. He whistled it from there all the
way to where I got off near to the old Penny Black
pub on Exmouth Market/Rosebery Avenue (can't
remember what it's called now – something like Le
Cafe Pretentious). I said to him, 'I haven't heard
Andrew Gold's "Never Let Her Slip Away" for about
twenty years. Cheers for that.'

'Was it by Andrew Gold?' he said. 'I just know the
tune. I had no idea who it was by.'

'You should listen to it and learn to whistle the
intro. It's got these lovely off the beat organ chords.'

'Thanks,' he said. 'I will.'

FALLING BACKWARDS IN THE PARK

It's angst time at the local playground. Should I let my daughter play on the big swings? The difference between the big swings and the little swings is one of falling backwards. At some point we have to let our child fall back and crack their head open on the hard playground floor of life.

On the big swings they stand up and talk about make-up and fashion, boys and music. In the little swings they are encased in hard metal frames and they cling on for dear life. But really it is us who are clinging on for dear life. Many fathers have said to me they can't let their kids go on the big swings because, erm, the kids are going to leave me one day and I'll die old, frail and alone in a retirement home.

We all have to face our own fears. Most Dads have buried anguished memories of being bullied on crappily run municipal playgrounds in the 1970s. If we can stand up to our imaginary bullies, we can let the kids move on. Here's a simple questionnaire to help.

Q. How do I know if my child is ready for the big swing?

A. Ask yourself, is your kid really happy? I mean, if your child is eighteen or over, you may be holding them back.

MANOR HOUSE

A pub built on the site of an ancient manor house, and near to Woodberry Down, Manor House was rebuilt in 1931. Jimi Hendrix played a gig here in May 1967. Not that long ago the pub was turned into a big Costcutter. Which suggests that human progress is not always linear and upward.

THE MUSEUM OF RECONSTITUTED CHARITY SHOP ART

17th May every year is my Thinking About Things day. It started back in 1988, not long after I'd arrived in London, when I spent the day in Alexandra Park thinking about what the fuck I was going to do with my life. Twelve years later, a year or so after we moved in here, on my Thinking About Things day I spent a couple of hours in the garden thinking about things, then went down the charity shop to think about things there for a while. On a shelf I saw a tacky print of Renoir's famous painting 'Luncheon of the Boating Party' so took it home and painted over it with a scene of the local East Reservoir*, a mile or so away from here, just below Woodberry Down.

This was my first painting for The Museum of Reconstituted Charity Shop Art. Whether it's a crappy Monet print, a bland Gainsborough in a plastic frame or a shiny Picasso with vinyl sheen, it can all be painted over with exciting scenes from everyday life such as tower blocks, old people and dodgy pubs. Somebody recently said that I was 'ennobling' these old pictures by painting over them. Ha.

That said, in recent years I've started to grow fond of the rubbish art I find in charity shops, to

The East Reservoir

the point at which I am now no longer sure whether my gritty urban-expressionist splatters are any better than the sentimentalised kitten pictures or soft-focus nature scenes in the frame. Perhaps I will think about this next 17th May.

*The patch of beautiful green scummy water in the foreground (OK – so it looks grey here) has now been filled in. The tower blocks are still there, though hopefully they are more architecturally sound than they appear in the picture.

54

I HEAR THE SOUND
OF MANDOLINS

It's Friday night at St Gabriel's Community Centre in Upper Holloway, North London. It's a 1970s redbrick trying-to-be-modernist structure that for a long time was the church hall for the large Irish community that lived and worked in the area around Holloway Road, Archway and Hornsey. Perhaps there was an older hall there before this one was built. Should I know about stuff like that? I certainly don't know where the church of St Gabriel's is.

We've just finished mandolin practice at Meitheal Cheoil, the North London Irish music school I frequent every Friday night. For the last few weeks we have been practising various things with a view to joining a mixed instrument group. It's called a *Grúpa Ceoil*. I can write it — only because I've checked the spelling on the internet — but I can't for the life of me say it. Seeing as I'm on the internet I'll check out the history of St Gabriel's church and hall, so you won't think I am uncaring about facts. OK, it's not far from the hall, in fact just on the other side of the railway line.

When we are practising mandolin on a Friday night I love to hear the sound of the trains rattling past.

SALUTING MAGPIES
ON A SUNNY MORNING

'Hello Mr Magpie!' I whispered, as I reached the
north-eastern sector of Clissold Park. Argh! Why do
I do this? I used to think it was a kind of commercial
TV brainwashing from the 1970s kids' show (*Magpie*
was presented by ex-hippies). But apparently it goes
back even further than the 70s, to our fear of the
devil or some Celtic deity. And anyway, in our family
we used to watch *Blue Peter*.

I'm convinced that it's something to do with
leprechauns.

WHAT GOOD ARE SNAILS?

'Just stamp on them,' says my wife. 'It's the most
humane thing you can do.' Being a socialist buddhist
(with a small 's' and a small 'b') I feel a bit squeamish
about this and that snails are somehow part of the
greater scheme of things. Granted, all they seem to
do is eat up all the little shoots and seedlings that I
have tried to grow. But although I don't like snails as a
species, individual snails are kind of cute, I suppose,
and I just don't have the heart to stomp on them.
I decided to try a more sneaky approach by putting
out beer for them to drown in. They are attracted to
the smell of real ale, apparently. After doing a test
on various brews I worked out that their favourite
was Prince Charles' Highgrove Duchy organic ale. I
wrote to Prince Charles asking him if he'd consider
going into a partnership. I'd draw the labels and
he could do, er, everything else. As usual with my
correspondence with royalty, I never heard back.

TWO PUB REVIEWS
(NOT VERY FACT-BASED)

THE ROCHESTER CASTLE, STOKE NEWINGTON, LONDON N19

London's no. 1 Wetherspoons pub, and there's a beer festival on. Turnpike, Broadside and Barn Owl for well under two quid. Crowds of old blokes talk about cricket and Guinness while pockets of cleaned-up 40-something ex-Clash fans get nostalgic for the days when Stoke Newington was cheap and you could get proper beer and a fight down the road at the Three Crowns.

The Tufnell Park Tavern, Tufnell Park Road, London N19

I've had some good nights in the Tufnell Park Tavern over the years. And a couple of crap ones as well. However, this review is really to register my displeasure when for a while the pub turned into something called Tufnell's — the name was up there in bright shiny metallic clubbiness. What kind of brand manager modern celeb-fixated small-brained philistine was let loose on this pub? It's in Tufnell Park. It's called the Tufnell Park Tavern. It should be so simple.

I didn't actually go into the pub on this occasion. I was on the top deck of the no. 4 bus with my two young sons.

'Why are you growling, Daddy?' asked my five-year-old.

What hope is there for us as a society, as a civilisation, as a species, when people make crazy decisions like this? How can we claim the idea of constant human progress when we change the names of pubs from something old and good to something modern and useless? When is the government going to sort out a proper Pub Czar* to get all these pubs to change their names back to the originals?

* Though the whole concept of a Czar might need looking at. I mean, the Czars didn't exactly cover themselves in glory, did they? They ended up as a sad pile of bones in a piece of rough ground. Maybe there should be a Czar Czar to rebrand the whole concept.

COMPOST IN MY RUCKSACK

A hike through the park with the rucksack to buy compost at the garden shop. The fences have finally been taken up on the top fields of the park and been rolled up into little biscuit shapes. It's like a reference to the round hay bales I used to see dotted around the countryside as a kid. The middle-aged bloke behind the counter starts telling me about Hull City's promotion and when he hears I'm a Leeds fan he talks about their downfall being down to the change from fast midfield running to a slow passing European-style game. He looks like Ena Sharples. Or perhaps Ena Sharples' older brother.

'North, south, east or west — it doesn't matter where you plant stuff. If you want it to grow, it'll grow.'

(That's a quote from the garden shop bloke, not Ena Sharples.)

PLANTS I DON'T KNOW THE
NAME OF: SPIDERY-LEAVED THING

A friend of mine grows these and took some cuttings
and gave them to me. Normally in these situations
I manage to kill the new plant in a matter of weeks,
but these pale green spidery leaved things seem to
be indestructible. What is it called? Adendum?
Benabus? Maranicle? Pandemania? Pantheisma?
Agamemnon? What is wrong with my memory?

Parsimony? Nastase? Pangea?
Nuneaton Grass? Pericles? Granolaria?

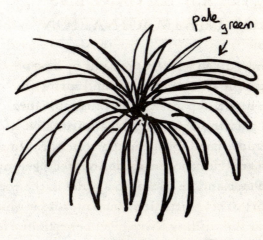

pale green

Alabama?

Agapanthus!

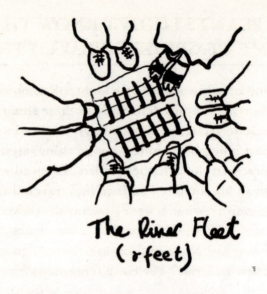

The River Fleet
(r feet)

PLEASURE GARDENS
OF THE IMAGINATION

A pub crawl/guided walk (supposedly by me –
ha!) around the sites of old wells and springs in
Clerkenwell, accompanied by an illustrator, two
architects, a mythological writer, a spiritualist, a
geologist and a small town country solicitor. Outside
the Coach and Horses one of the architects gets out
some blue tape and we stick it to a grille in the road
as some sort of crazy artistic statement, under which
we can hear the rushing River Fleet beneath our feet.
The illustrator has really nice blue nail varnish on
her toes.

NATURE WATCH:
GARDEN BIRDS

Nothing beats the sound of nature in your back garden, especially the world of our feathered friends. Not so long ago, I was sitting at the kitchen table procrastinating over something or other when there was a crack on the pane behind me. I looked outside and saw that a small brown bird had smacked into the big glass kitchen door. Oh my god, it's Mrs Blackbird! Mr and Mrs B would make regular visits to our lawn, where they'd find big tasty worms (and old tennis balls etc). But the bird was smaller than a blackbird. Luckily, I have a Ladybird book on hand for most occasions, and the Ladybird *Garden Birds* showed that this was most likely a young blackbird. By the time I'd got outside the bird was dead. It was buried with full honours in the animals' graveyard – alongside Stripe the goldfish and a couple of mice.

MAGIC

ORANGE

THE MAGIC ORANGE

I was travelling on the tube, something I don't like to
do all that often, being an ardent bus/walk person.
It was the Victoria Line heading north, and we'd just
got to Oxford Circus. Piles of people got on. One of
them was a frail looking old man, possibly Chinese.
I offered him my seat and he smiled and nodded and
smiled again then sat down. He rummaged around in
his bag and pulled out a really big orange.

'Thank you. Special orange.' He smiled and
nodded, and handed me the orange.

'Thanks very much.' I said. Wow. I had been given
a *magic* orange. This orange had special powers – I
decided it might possibly change my life for the
better. I should point out that he didn't tell me it was
magic. I just *knew*.

Not long after this incident I formed a country
band along with a few mates and my wife, and called
it Magic Orange. I told them all about the old man
and the orange and they nodded. We went on to play
about five gigs at crappy little pub venues, and then
we split up.

If I hadn't met that old bloke on the tube that
day, who knows what adventures I might have missed.
Thank you, old (possibly Chinese) man.

CICADAS SINGING
IN FINSBURY PARK

A dazzlingly hot day. Sunshine, heat and exotic
sounds abound in Finsbury Park border country.
The distant, ever-present, burglar alarm buzz from
a couple of streets away is like an incessant cicadas'
song. As the day wears on, a heat haze appears over
the old Hornsey Wood on the brow of the park. The
alarm fades away and instead I hear the sweet sound
of drills, talk radio in the air, and builders swearing
at each other.

THE STONE

As I was flicking through the Stoke Newington OS
map from 1868 (it's a gripping read) I noticed that,
north of the avenue and embankment that was once
the New River, was a stone. No other explanation.
Just 'stone'. Was it a milestone, like the one on
the bend of the New River near St Mary's church?
Maybe this is the same stone and it was moved
into an enclosed area for safe keeping. Or was the
'stone' something else, something older still? Like a
Neolithic marker which, though long gone, still gives
off a strange magnetic pull that attracts summertime
Frisbee throwers and the Turkish football team (it's
near the spot where they do their windsprints).

There must be a historian around who knows
these things, some Professor of Invisible Ancient
Stones of North London at University College.

RELUCTANT GARDENER

With spring in the air it's that time of year when I order loads of packets of seeds off the internet then stuff them in a drawer and forget about them (in a parallel universe I have all kinds of interesting native plants and wildflowers growing). Around now a wide variety of brightly coloured perennials will start to appear, particularly the punctured beach ball, the one-legged Rapunzel Barbie, the ride-on fire engine with a really annoying noise and the cheap Spacehopper substitute that gets used as a punchbag. But I have been doing a bit of work, installing a section of wooden sleeper near the outside toilet where I can rest my radio.

CHIP PAN MAN

Not long after we moved into the street in the
late 90s a strange looking man with wire-rimmed
spectacles came to the door one night. He seemed
frantic with worry. He'd accidentally spilled oil from
the chip pan onto his daughter and needed to get
her to hospital but the ambulance was going to take
too long. He needed a taxi but had no money for the
phone call – could we help? I told him to come in
and use our phone but he was reluctant, saying he'd
prefer the money. I got confused, then he got a bit
cross and headed off.

Then, a couple of years later, there was a knock at
the door. It was the same man, the same wire-rimmed
specs. Before I had a chance to apologise for my
previous parsimony and ask how his daughter was he
blurted out, 'I spilled chip pan oil onto my daughter
and I need money for a taxi to get her to hospital. Can
you help me?' He must be a careless cook, I thought.

A bit more recently I was walking up the hill from
Blackstock Road, up Highbury Park, when a man
appeared from a side street, looking very perplexed.

'I've had my wallet stolen and I need to get back
to my family tonight. Can you help me with some
money for the train ticket?'

'Where do you live?' I asked.

'Er, Hertfordshire.'

I looked him in the eyes. He looked vaguely familiar,
a worried expression, wire-rimmed spectacles . . .

LOCAL SLUGS

Looking south-east through the slats in the blind, I can see four policemen with black padded waistcoats – the kind of thing their mums would have put together if they'd starred as Mr Bumble in a school production of *Oliver!* – standing around outside a house. The occupant, a loud-voiced alcoholic lady of no fixed age, has wandered off in the direction of Blackstock Road. I go back to my work and rely on the keen eye of my wife, who sits by the window and keeps me updated on events.

An hour or so later there is a massive boom and the walls and windows shake. A Pickfords ('The Careful Movers') removal lorry has driven fast over the traffic calming ramps outside our house and sped off in the direction of Stoke Newington, smashing into the tarmac every fifty yards or so. This is the kind of noise that has sent an old bloke at the end of the road into such a rage that he has recently threatened to start supporting the BNP.

It's a cold/hot/cold/cold/hot weather day. We're all waiting for more rain. The slugs will be out to feast on the shoots in my herb garden, but tonight I'll be ready for them with some handily placed trays of Budvar beer. Two bottles for me, one for the slugs.

GOLDEN SKIES OVER HOLLOWAY

The daffodils are out in Clissold Park. Squat dogs run round and through them.

'Kaiser! Butch! Over here!' shouts an angry-looking man with little hair. The sky over Lower Holloway is golden but greyness is descending as the wind picks up. A blue plastic bag joins us on our walk and keeps pace for a while before blowing up into the branches of a tree.

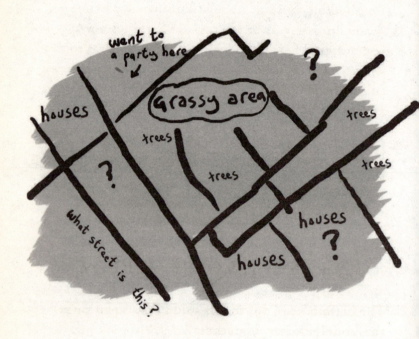

I DON'T REALLY KNOW
THIS AREA VERY WELL

Ten years or so ago, on a hot summer morning,
I headed off on foot through Finsbury Park then
headed north-east, into an area that I had never
encountered before. The plan for my trip was to go
swimming at Archway pool. I like the feeling of being
completely lost in London; it excites me that I can
still have no idea where I am, and in these Victorian
streets of three-storey terraced houses I almost lost
all sense of direction. Once I entered this strangely
still atmosphere, I forgot why I had set off and just
meandered along the streets, cutting into each new
one in turn.

Eventually I came out somewhere on Hornsey
Road around where it becomes Crouch End Hill,
near a little model shop, where I bought some Alpini
Regiment 1:72 scale plastic soldiers and a Grumman
Wildcat model (a 1970s Frog kit). I long ago gave
up model making, of course, but I still look out for
Grumman Wildcats — it was the first model I bought
when I was eight, and I always love the Proustian rush
of finding a new one.

After that I went for a coffee nearby, then
sauntered home back along Hornsey Road towards
Drayton Park. It was only as I got close to my house
that I realised I had completely forgotten about the
swimming.

LOCAL WILDLIFE: ZEN AND THE ART OF MOTORCYCLE MENTALISTS

Wandering through frantic yet beautiful Holloway on a blazing afternoon I come to the junction of Camden Road, pleased with myself for managing to get this far without purchasing any second-hand office furniture (it's an addiction, you see). Suddenly a small motorbike appears on the pedestrian island in the middle of the road. Its owner, a mad-looking heat-crazed red haired bloke with a very red face, is screaming at another guy who apparently has just 'laughed' at his bike. It's all a bit over the top – lots of 'come on then you slag' and 'who's laughing now!!?' etc etc. Tiredly, I put my hand on the biker's arm as he tries to 'run over' the teaser and say, as calmly as possible in my best hippy voice, 'Hey man, there are kids. In prams.'

Mad Biker turns his gaze to me and screams at the top of his voice 'Yeah!?!?' Worried that he might now try to run me over, I quickly walk away and head for the nearest second-hand furniture shop.

NOT MINDFUL
OF HEDGECUTTING

It's one o'clock on a Saturday afternoon, and time is dragging slowly. The heavy heat of the early summer day is pulling my heart down. I sweep leaves as my neighbour cuts the hedges on our street. He asks me about my car. Am I happy with it? I sweep slowly.

'I'll probably need to replace mine soon,' he says as he strips the leaves from behind the bike shed.

For some reason my disembodied mind is elsewhere — I am part of a revolutionary folk-rock band travelling in a train across the USA, acoustic guitars by our sides.

'I probably should have got a Ford,' he says, and turns the hedgecutter back on.

HIGHBURY CORNER

At the southern end of Highbury proper and on the
border of Islington and Canonbury, this used to be
a 'real' corner, but a VI bomb in World War Two
and then council and British Rail developments led
to the demolition of the grand old Highbury station
and the building of the roundabout and associated
charity shops, fried chicken fast food outlets and
exceptionally slow traffic.

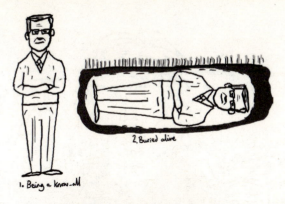

1. Being a know-all
2. Buried alive

BETTER SHED THAN,
ER, SOMETHING . . .

The lid of our storage box falling on my head
destroys several thousand of my brain cells a day
and stops me remembering what I don't like about
gardening. So finally I ordered a proper shed
from Argos, somewhere nice and warm where the
delicate creatures of the garden (i.e. me) can survive
the cold afternoons and listen to football on the
radio. Putting a flatpacked shed together is mightily
difficult and possibly one of the most traumatic
things you'll ever have to do in your life. Luckily for
me, one of our neighbours is a shed expert.

'In my day we built them from scratch. Have you
levelled out the ground?' He's full of great advice.
I expect I'll have to get rid of him in the garden.
Like in that film *The Vanishing* (not the version with Jeff
Bridges).

I was starting to like the shed when it was an idea.
Now that it's real, I've sort of gone off it.

HIPPY

SEASONAL HAIR

It's the start of spring — and here I'm referring to
Imbolc, from the old Irish/Gaelic calendar, which
refers to the beginning of February — and I've just
had all my hair cut off again.* It's the same every year
but still startles and confuses people who've forgotten
that I looked like this twelve months earlier. It
disconcerts local barbers as well, who have to work
bloody hard for their money.

   I treat my hair how a farmer treats his crops, and
I've been running this annual system for a decade
and a half. At some point during the year I start to
look like a Viking hippy, or maybe late period Jim
Morrison. Eventually I have it all cut off (used to be
a number two or three, now just a crop) so I can be

U-BOAT OFFICER

reintroduced into polite society, at which point I look a bit like a WWII German U-Boat captain.**

I am like a method actor preparing for some sci-fi film part in which Jim Morrison doesn't die but goes back in time to captain a German U-Boat, or something like that. ***

* Usually there will be a run of Siberian weather settling on North London just after I become a skinhead.

** My family also suggested it's like a journey from a *Time Team* hippy weapons-specialist to Mr Incredible (the gone-to-seed version, of course).

** Film producers – phone me!

THE FIGHT

I was walking east, through the windy border country, when I saw in the distance a few people standing at the side of the street. They were watching a man hit a woman repeatedly in the face. I quickened to a trot then found my legs going faster until I found myself standing between the man and the woman. The man — I call him a 'man' but he was less than that — shouted at me to get out of the way, that I was an idiot and that he was 'gonna do' me. Another woman arrived and helped to shield the victim. The angry nutcase went back to his car, then returned and said he'd 'fucking kill' us, then tried to hit her again.

By the time the police arrived the brave warrior with the flash car had scarpered. It turned out that the woman had been walking her pram across a zebra crossing when he had nearly run her over in his car. He'd then jumped out and tried to beat her up at her sheer effrontery at not leaping out of the way.

A while later I learned that he had escaped charge because he had witnesses — who he, presumably, had threatened to hit repeatedly in the face if they crossed him — who said that he'd been somewhere else at the time. I hope he has nightmares about it, like the woman's little girl, but I doubt it.

FOX NEWS:
THE SOUND OF FOXES HAVING SEX

Although I spent my childhood in the countryside I never heard a fox. There'd be the odd kid who lived in the woods who'd tell us of their haunting, shrieking cries. I rarely saw one, either – now and again when a hunt was on nearby a vision of red would dash across our path and we would lie to the chasing huntsmen that we hadn't seen anything. But now, in the never ending quiet Victorian streets of North London, I see foxes every other night, often two or three together. And at night they can be heard in the garden. When I first heard this sound I thought it was the ghosts of evil witches attacking a cat but apparently, according to my know-all neighbour, it's the sound of foxes having sex. I'm happy for the foxes, but I fixed the hole in the fence so they can have sex in my know-all neighbour's garden from now on.

GOODBYE CHERRY BLOSSOM

The cherry blossom of Kingsbridge House, on Lordship Road, has gone, blown in the wind towards Seven Sisters Road. Up there, amid the concrete they would have been greedily awaiting the annual visit of the pale pink swarms. The wind also trapped a red plastic kite in the branches of a Clissold Park plane tree, like a sliver of raw flesh hanging on thin ribs.

My kids find more blossom at the side of the road on Grazebrook Road. I explain that it's probably 40 per cent dog urine but they don't care, and run down the path with it, letting it fly out of their hands behind them.

'IN NATURE EVERYONE HAS A JOB'

I have been having worries about killing the snails again. The idea of leaving beer out for them is that I believed it wouldn't be me killing them, it would be the beer. I am not proud of what I have learned about myself during this snail episode. I do not have the courage of my convictions. Sometimes even part-time hobbies test us and give us an insight into what makes us tick.

'In nature everyone has a job,' says the old lady next door, standing on a stepladder and watching me. 'Snails eat dead vegetation.'

But they don't just eat dead vegetation. They eat live vegetation. Their role seems to be to make sure no young plants survive and leave more garden free for snails to hang out in. Loads of our kids' books have stories about snails. Sammy Snail in the garden. Munched on lettuce. But an evil gardener (like Mr McGregor in Beatrix Potter's *Peter Rabbit*) chases after Sammy and only fails to catch him thanks to the ingenuity of Sammy's garden friends, such as Steve Spider, Laura Ladybird and Selena Slug.

SUMMER
(unlikely to be
a heatwave)

PLANTS I DON'T KNOW THE NAME OF: LITTLE FLOWER, GROWING IN THE WALL

This is probably one of my favourite plants in the whole garden. It's a tiny little flower — no more than a couple of inches high — growing out the upper bricks in one of the low walls at the back of the house. There's something about its indomitable spirit and creativity that I love. It's an optimistic little flower. Who needs soil when you have old London bricks?

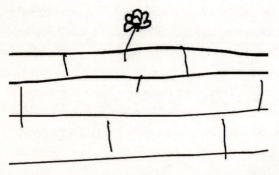

MY FAVOURITE TREE

Everyone has a favourite tree. Don't they? Like a
soulmate, but with bark and leaves and squirrels
living in it and dogs pissing against the side of it.
Mine is a small but perfectly formed horse chestnut
in the northern, lower slopes of Clissold Park. It's
always the first tree to be in full leaf in the spring
and as soon as the sun comes out I ache to sit under
its leaves and read inspirational nature poetry,
especially of people like Michael Donaghy, Gary
Snyder, Basho, Walt Whitman (well, for a couple of
pages or so before I start screaming). I never do, of
course, being always in far too much of a hurry to get
somewhere else. But when I am at that 'somewhere
else' destination I start thinking that I'd rather be
sitting underneath my favourite tree.

Tomorrow. I'll sit under my favourite tree *tomorrow*.

THE FAIR

The fair has probably been coming to the southern
triangle of the park for a hundred years or more.
I think this parcel of land used to be part of a
common. On one level a trip to the fair lets us see
our neighbours in another setting but I am also left
with a feeling of achievement after not getting sick
on the big dipper. Well, it wasn't actually very big. It
was a small dipper for little kids and crap dads. Last
time I went to the fair I got sick on the waltzer. In
my defence I'm sure I had a low-level bug. Or maybe
it was a dodgy pint or two of ale. (Good job I never
wanted to be a fighter pilot – though it would have
been a funny story for *Victor* comic; a fighter pilot
who kept puking in his cockpit.)

A NEW UNDERGROUND RIVER

Amazing news. I've recently learned about an underground river that flows from Highbury down into the Hackney Brook Valley. Usually I spot these streams when I see cans of extra strong lager scattered about on the surface, but in this case there was a whole off-licence. I was buying a few bottles of beer at Highbury Vintners and commented on the strange slope of the floor in the shop, which seemed to counter the slope of Highbury Hill.

'That's because there's a river that flows under the shop,' said the owner. 'It goes through here and underneath the church.' I expressed an interest in starting to go to mass, then fiddled about with the real ales before announcing to the whole shop: 'I've written a book about underground rivers.'

The shopkeeper was not fazed. 'Bloody Highbury. Every time I bring up some topic of conversation, one of our customers will go, "I've written a book about that".'

HOW TO CATCH MICE

My wife is terrified of mice and goes crazy whenever she sees one. By the time I get up from the sofa and put down my glass of wine the mouse is long gone thanks to her howling screams. One of the problems is that I never actually see the mice, and it did occur to me that perhaps my wife is inventing the mice just to make sure I don't get too comfortable on the sofa watching repeats of *Black Books* on TV.

Whereas my wife thinks of mice as vermin, I take a different view. To me they are just part of nature, and with this in mind I have constructed humane ways of catching them involving bottles of port and nice bits of cheese from The Fromagerie up the road. In a way I am trying to befriend the mice, saying to them, 'It's cool to be a mouse, but do you think you could be a mouse somewhere else for a while, please?' I know this is a bit mouseist, but anything for an easy life.

I did eventually catch a live mouse. I put it in a brown paper bag along with a nice bit of cheese from The Fromagerie (Lincolnshire Poacher) and walked it to the local park, where I set it free with its piece of cheese near a big pile of leaves.

It probably got back to the house before me.

ARSENAL FULLBACKS TRY TO CHANGE THE WORLD IN A NIGHT

Lee Dixon came to our local pub
and tried to convert us all
to the cause of International socialism.
'You're too late mate,' said the landlord.
'We had that Nigel Winterburn in here last night.
We're all Buddhists now.'

THE NEWSPAPER DILEMMA

On days like this when I'm really busy playing Operation with my daughter I'm faced with a dilemma. Do I go to the nearest newspaper shop, where the head guy doesn't really speak English (apart from 'hello' and 'yes boss') or go a bit further away to get my papers from Dursun? Dursun and his family are interesting talkative types. But his shop is about 30 yards further away.

I used to go to Dursun's all the time, but now I try to save time by going to the shop that's nearest. What I think I'm going to do with this saved time I haven't really considered. It's only about an extra minute. And I only buy three newspapers a week these days. That's three minutes a week, 156 minutes a year. Could I write a novel in the time available? Yes, in theory. In 156 minutes I reckon I could do around 1,500 words. So for a shortish 80,000-word novel, it'd take me 53 years. So I'll have finished it by the time I'm 93.

I think it's a worthwhile project and something to keep me occupied when I'm an old dodderer. I'm going to give it a working title of *The Newspaper Novel*.

By the way, today I persuaded my wife to get the paper, as I didn't want to leave the house. Some of the plastic bones from Operation have gone missing and I need to do a scan of the living room. I think my daughter has deliberately hidden them because she knows they are my lucky bones.

Waterlow Park

Walking under trees and looking down at London, time slows down. In summer you can sit in among the wildflowers and long grass and watch the sky. Then you can quickly roll down the hill and you're back in Archway.

THE SHREDDER

I'm as worried about identity theft as the next person, which is why I invested in this high-performance shredder, bought from my favourite stationers on Blackstock Road (a bit of genius cross-selling by the stationer when I'd gone in to buy a pen). When boxed up it fits perfectly into the back of my store cupboard behind my practice amp. I've had it for nearly three years but only used it twice, both times to eradicate some really bad draft lyrics for political folk songs that I'd written on the back of my VISA card statements.

If someone does steal my identity I would suggest they get hold of a shredder as well, to help protect their new identity. Though come to think of it, if it's possible to steal an identity then one could just as easily steal an identity back. That's not theft, it's identity justice.

I think I'll tear out this page and shred it.

Tear or cut here

THE OLD TIN BOX FACTORY ON BLACKSTOCK ROAD

In my post-pub dreams the old deserted tin box factory on Blackstock Road was going to be turned into something exciting. Any day now. In my dreams it has been:

1) A writers' retreat with fountains and personalised minibars
2) A cafe for nymphomaniac jazz chicks
3) A zoo for put-upon grey squirrels
4) A cinema for stay-at-home dads
5) A swimming pool for people with dodgy knees
6) A museum of cheese

Unfortunately I always dreamed these things but never did anything about them. The bulldozers have been and the old deserted tin box factory on Blackstock Road is a few piles of browny-yellow brick. Which of my ideas will become reality? Or will it become just another shite block of modernist flats?

FOX NEWS:
THE THREE-LEGGED FOX

I love foxes. Or, rather, I love seeing foxes in the
street, as they trot nonchalantly past you smiling
and saying, 'Good evening to you, Sir.' Well, of
course, they don't say that — but they certainly think
it. They are very polite in the street. It's only in back
gardens that they resort to fighting, having loud sex,
bursting plastic footballs and digging up plants. They
are garden devils, street angels. So I don't like foxes
making themselves too comfortable in our garden.
I'm such a NFIMBY.

Recently I saw a fox curled up having a well-earned
snooze in one corner of the garden so I went out to
shoo it away. It got up reluctantly, looking at me with
the same expression my oldest son has when I tell
him it's bed time: 'Aaaaaawwww, Daaaaad!' And then
I noticed the fox only had three legs. 'That's pretty
cool,' I thought. He was perhaps a fox version of the
ancient Irish one-legged god Lugh, who was famed
for making stuff out of bronze — weapons, trinkets,
things to sell at a craft market on a rainy Saturday.
Or the fox could be the power animal of the three-
legged stool that I encountered near the burning
shoe a few years ago.

More worryingly, he could also be part of a clever
marketing campaign for the not-very-well-known-
in-fact-I-had-to-Google-them American rock
band, Three Legged Fox.

BIGFOOT

Last night I put my foot through the bath. I simply stood up to get a towel and my foot just went straight through, sending water cascading through the bathroom and down into the kitchen. There's now a big hole and two bits of bath — some kind of twin-skin acrylic resin stuff. I still can't explain it — I'm not that heavy (about twelve stone). Maybe it's like a karate-type thing where you focus all your power into one part of your body. Don't think I'll tell the insurance people about my copy of *The Power of the Internal Martial Arts* by Bruce Kumar Frantzis. In fact, I think I'll store it in the loft for a couple of weeks, until this Foot Through Bath incident is forgotten.

AVOIDING THE GAMBLER

On days like this when I'm really busy it's essential that I manage to avoid the gambler. Whenever I bump into the gambler he tends to take up a blocking position that is impossible to counter. The gambler's favourite topics of conversation are:

1) The speed bumps in the road that lorries drive over, which keeps him awake at night

2) The inevitability of the UK becoming a Muslim state

3) Women, and how he doesn't have much luck with them

A while ago I rushed out to the corner shop to buy some herbs for some fish I was cooking. The gambler must have been hiding in undergrowth in his front garden for he suddenly popped out in front of me, and started to tell me about his relationship with Michael Flatley, the *Riverdance* bloke. He even had a photo of the two of them in his jacket pocket.

ME: Got to go. I'm in a hurry.

THE GAMBLER: You're always in a hurry. You need to relax a bit more.

Now and again I will try to predict where I'll meet him. I'll change direction at the last minute, but there he'll be. He must have some kind of high-tech sonar equipment built into his fedora.

'In fifteen years' time we will all be Muslim, you know.'

PLANTS I DON'T KNOW THE NAME OF: WILDFLOWERS/WEEDS GROWING IN THE PAVEMENT

On a late spring afternoon I encountered a Mad Max-like figure on our road, covered in protective gear and with a liquid-filled canister on his back. He was spraying the pavement with what I presumed must be weedkiller.

    - What about the wildflowers? I said.

    - Eh? What? He turned around.

    - You know, biodiversity. What's wrong with a few wildflowers growing in the pavement? It's good for bees.

    - It's my job, he muttered, then shrugged.

    I wanted to tell him about all the different wildflowers (or 'weeds' as they are usually known) but I didn't know their names so I just sighed. He continued with his spraying.

PIRATES IN THE PARK

Today I was King of the Dragon Pirates and we were escaping to Narnia (I think) via the track on the north side of Clissold Park, being chased by Giant Pirates. Giant Pirates are bad and Dragon Pirates are, generally, thought to be good — at least in the world of six- and three-year-olds. There were a lot of empty cans of extra strong lager dotted around — a well-known vice of the Giant Pirates.

Then we all went home to watch telly.

dragons

giant

NORTH LONDON
FATHERS' TRIATHLON

One of the main reasons to stay fit is so you can run for a bus and catch it. I've always prided myself on being able to catch just about any bus I want — even if I miss a stop I'll sometimes run for the next one. In the last couple of years this has been getting harder. But recently I tried the North London Fathers' Triathlon, in which one runs for a bus after completing two even more gruelling events, as follows:

1) Getting to school to pick up kids while pushing a pram when you're a mile away and five minutes behind schedule.

2) Trying to find every overdue library book in the house within a fifteen-minute period (at advanced level, there'll be two or three toddler books hidden behind bookshelves).

If this was introduced into the Olympics it would be a constant gold medal bonanza for Britain (North London doesn't have its own team — yet).

THE OLD LADY'S GARDEN

The old lady who lived in the house before us had
been here for fifty years. Her lovely garden was full
of peonies on the day we first saw it. We stood on the
lawn looking around at all the plants, then looking at
the big sky, and knew we were going to live here.

CLISSOLD PARK BOWLING GREEN

I've been flicking through *Wonderful London* (ed. St John Adcock), a three-volume set from 1926. This is the bowling green before it stopped being a bowling green and became a teen alcopops awareness centre. If this picture was taken now there'd be a mad-looking bloke with a bull terrier striding towards the camera shouting obscenities.

'STOKE NEWINGTON IN SUMMER-TIME: THE BOWLING GREEN AT CLISSOLD PARK
A long journey through the dreary Kingsland Road and on through Stoke Newington brings one to Church Street, a curious survival in the surrounding villadom. There are old houses and a small sixteenth-century church, mellow with years, and farther on the fifty-two green acres of Clissold Park, through whose ordered lawns runs the New River. Beyond the bowling green is the spire of the modern parish church, built by Sir Gilbert Scott to replace the old one which was put up when the congregation was that of a country village.'

THE OLD HOUSE
ON HORNSEY ROAD

Nobody I know seems to know much about the
old house on Hornsey Road. I go past it every
Friday evening, on my way to my mandolin class.
Distinguishing features? The windows are quite
ornate, and there is some scrubby grass in the front
garden, which looks like it should be for a cottage in
the Lake District. But it's actually a small car park.

The old house on Hornsey Road looks like it was
part of a much older row of villas but is now the
only survivor of (... erm, probably the early-mid
19th century, but leave this bit blank for now – I'll
do some research on it at the Hornsey Local History
Library. Actually, I bet I won't).

FOOTBALL KID

On Lordship Road a thin figure walks slowly
along the pavement bouncing a leather football.
Occasionally he does a few juggles on his knee and
feet and I think to myself this is good, this is what
football is all about. He then kicks the ball onto the
trunk of an old tree on the other side of the road,
narrowly avoiding hitting a white van that is speeding
past. Further up he confronts a group of Jewish
women standing in a group and threatens to kick
the ball at them, while making strange Lon Chaney
gurning faces at them. Then he stands in the road
kicking the ball in the air. A car brakes suddenly
and the driver leaps out of his car, shouting and
swearing.

Penny Rimbaud, Crass

THE NORTH LONDON COMPENDIUM OF LOST THINGS: THE VORTEX

It had been a while since I walked down Stoke Newington Church Street, but I was shocked to see that the old Vortex building has gone. I kind of half expected that the Vortex would have been saved at the last minute (like in the movies) by a kindly anarchist-philanthropist, and was once again happily jumping to the sounds of atonal improvised sax playing.

But the Vortex had gone, to be replaced by a load of scaffolding. No more will I come staggering home at half past two in the morning, dying for a waz, and be suddenly seduced inside by the strange wails of freeform jazz. No more will I be able to ruin a perfectly good evening by suggesting, 'Hey, let's go and see Penny Rimbaud out of Crass!' In its glory days there was also a rest home downstairs for all those lost texts about structural film theory and feminist cultural critiques. Has the Vortex by any chance been put in the British Museum?

FINSBURY PARK

Finsbury Park has a few old pubs, a pound shop and a variety of fried chicken outlets. And, of course, a nice big park where I used to take my daughter to the swings. It has somehow escaped the gentrification happening in other parts of North London. Unlike Highbury, Stoke Newington or Crouch End it's not based on an old Middlesex village but grew up around the new (as of 19th century) rail intersection near Stroud Green Farm and Hornsey Wood.

It's great that Victorian campaigners saved the park for future Stone Roses fans (and dads with little kids).

LOCAL WILDLIFE: MAGPIES, SALUTING AND DE-SALUTING

This morning I saw a magpie and, without thinking, saluted it. 'Good morning, Mr Magpie!'

Then another magpie appeared from behind a tree trunk and I realised they were a pair. And I attempted to de-salute the first magpie. But it's tricky. How does one do this? It's obviously some kind of uninstall procedure. But do you say the words backwards? Or do you explain in depth to the magpie that you are taking back your greeting? Or do you let the greeting stand?

Trouble was, I wasn't wearing my glasses. As I got closer I realised they weren't magpies but rooks.

Action points: 1. Attempt to access rational brain. 2. Get eyes tested.

THE WORLD IS
CHANGING TOO FAST

In the latest *Balamory* on the BBC CBeebies channel
that's been specially designed for stay-at-home
fathers, Archie (the inventor) went round to Josie
Jump's house, but Josie, the pretty sporty one,
is now played by a different actress so I couldn't
concentrate. I kept pointing at the screen and
shouting 'what?' as if trying to embarrass an
annoying queue jumper. The strange thing was, even
Archie the inventor hadn't noticed.

'What?' I said again.

'What's wrong, Dad?' said my daughter.

'Josie's different,' I said.

'So what?' she shrugged.

'But. But...'

Kids don't understand. Where has the other
actress gone?

TATRAN (SLOVAK SHOP)

On the borders of N5 and N4 is the quiet corner
of Finsbury Park Road and Mountgrove Road. The
latter used to have a variety of shops: accordion
seller, antiques, bikes, two Chinese takeaways, design
agency, a Sylvanian Families franchise. Some of these
have gone to be replaced by apartments but new
businesses keep appearing; latterly a 1940s furniture
emporium and a computer repair shop.

When Tatran appeared on this corner two or three
years ago it seemed perfect for a street which for
a long time has been threatening to become more
interesting. A few times I took my work there and
sat in the back of the cafe, where you could get away
from it all and sip virtually tasteless yet strangely
enjoyable Slovakian milky coffee. The place was
usually manned by attractive Slovak girls who would
sit at a table near the window leafing through what
looked like the Argos catalogue and *Heat* magazine.

But now Tatran is no more. It closed for the
summer holidays and never reopened. At the time
of writing the place is being done up – the peachy
orange is now brick red and the handwritten 'Slovak
Shop' sign painted over. Where will we get Slovakian
chocolate bars now, then? Or Slovakian vacuum-
packed frankfurters? Or idiosyncratic Slovakian
biscuits? And where, in the whole of London, will we
get virtually tasteless yet strangely enjoyable Slovakian
milky coffee?

THE NORTH LONDON
COMPENDIUM OF LOST THINGS:
MY AMAZING EUROPEAN
PHOTO ALBUM

My Amazing European Photo Album charted
my progress through various western European
countries in the autumn of 1989. At the very
moment Europe was changing and the iron curtain
was coming down, there was me having my photo
taken with various gurning characters in bars.

Over two decades ago I decided to go off to live
in South America for a while and so one night just
before I left I said to my wife, who was living in a flat
above the big launderette in Blackstock Road, 'Can

you look after my Amazing European Photo Album?'
I can't remember her answer — we were both pretty
drunk — but after that I stopped worrying about
the photo album because it had now become her
responsibility.

When I returned, my wife (actually, she wasn't my
wife then or even my girlfriend, but I'd obviously
worked out that I could dump responsibilities at
her door then blame her if things went wrong)
had moved to a new flat in a different part of town
and claimed not to know anything about the photo
album. So I'd lost it.

Every time I go up to Finsbury Park to buy some
stationery or bagels I pass the launderette, but it has
never occurred to me to see if My Amazing European
Photo Album is still there. Until now. I saw a couple
go into the flat the other day and thought they looked
like reasonable people. I think I will write them a
formal letter.

WELCOME TO ANATOLIA

Every once in a while one of those perfect North
London early summer weekend days comes along
and today's the day. We all stroll over to the park to
try out the Anatolian festival. It's like a cross between
an old fashioned village fete and an agricultural
show, except with belly dancers, kebabs and slogans
on posters that I don't understand. We buy kebab
and chips and sit on the grass. There is some kind
of wrestling going on further up the park. The
kids can't believe how exciting it is. My wife meets
someone from work and we all chat while listening
to a left-field Anatolian trumpet band. My daughter
leans over and says to me, 'Dad, is Anatolia in Turkey
or is Turkey in Anatolia?' and I wish I hadn't mucked
around so much in my Geography O-Level class.

THE SNAIL HOUSE

I'm fascinated by snails because I can't kill them.
They have a strange power over me. A quick look
back over art history confirms that many artists were
gardeners who had grown frustrated with snails. For
centuries people have put snails in art. That's because
they stamped on the actual snail and felt guilty about
it. Snail shells have a kind of swirly pattern like the
ancient Celtic motifs. Miro used snail patterns, as
did Picasso. And Antoni Gaudi used real snails to
decorate his cathedral in Barcelona, then had them
turned to stone by an evil sprite. At least, that's what
our tour guide said. I think.

The great garden philosopher, Epicurus, had
lots to say about various aspects of gardening. But
he said nothing about snails, which suggests that he
hated them. Or had already killed them all. But I
have decided to let the snails live. You get loads of
flies where the pulped snail/shell mix lies rotting in
the sun. A sunflower — their favourite food — is, after
all, no more important than a snail. So I built a snail
house, a multi-floor snail complex with lots of green
leaves thrown in and decided to embrace the world of
snails rather than destroy it.

LOCAL WILDLIFE:
THICK-NECKED BLOKE
WITH A DOG

One morning I was on my way back from the child-
minder's on the other side of the park, child safely
deposited, when I noticed something interesting.
At the end of the tree-lined bank that used to carry
the New River, as the path turns sharply northwards,
there is a small fenced-off area with a sign saying
'Dog Free Zone'. Traditionally this has been the
only part of the park where your kids can mess about
on their hands and knees without fear of getting
covered in dog shit. But this morning a tall, thick-
necked bloke with a skinhead was standing on his
own, staring out, while his fat-headed Pitbull/
Staffordshire/Thick Terrier-cross was running
around attacking the grass, looking for a place to
piss.

I went up to him, with the fence between us. 'You
know this is a dog free zone, don't you?'

'What? What?!'

I sighed inwardly. 'You've got the whole park. Why
do you have to go in there with your dog?'

His face started to go a deep pink. And not from
embarrassment. He seemed quite outraged that
someone could just walk up to him in a park and talk
to him like this. I knew what was coming.

'You can't tell me what to do.'

And he was probably thinking to himself, was this why we fought the Nazis, so some park Nazi could try and tell me where my dog can and can't shit? He was thinking that I was trying to curtail his freedom – freedom, obviously, meaning that he should be able to do what the hell he likes, where the hell he likes and sod everyone else.

It's a peculiarly Anglo-Saxon form of freedom, beloved of tabloid newspapers, right-wing politicians and stupid people in pubs. A braver, or should I say more resilient man than me would have stayed and argued the toss and (obviously) eventually had a fight with this twat. But I just muttered 'wanker', shook my head and walked on across the park.

GETTING WAYLAID
WHILE BUYING DIY SUPPLIES

Yesterday I went out onto Blackstock Road with
the specific task of buying a replacement blade
for my hacksaw. A nice, simple, job — there are
three hardware shops within half a mile or so, so
it shouldn't have been too difficult. Yet when I
returned to the house all I had managed to buy were
some really pretty little plants with delicate purple
flowers. Somehow I had got waylaid. Somewhere
along the way my face — set in a hard, determined,
focused frown that said 'hacksaw blades' — changed to
a smile of wonderment at the pretty flowers I saw and
I forgot all about my important DIY task.

I need to cut a metal curtain rail. But the flowers
really are very lovely.

BUYING A GOOD COAT

For years I've been meaning to buy myself a good
coat. This year I had a decent budget and went up
the West End, but with no success. On my way home,
walking along Holloway Road, I went into that mad
little second-hand clothes shop near the college and
picked up a mint condition tweedy overcoat that
looks like it used to belong to Jacques Chirac and was
made by some posh tailor in Paris. It only cost £20,
and now I am hooked. I've a feeling that this same
shop has some of François Mitterand's old shirts,
a Georges Pompidou suit and a very tiny 1998-era
Manchester United shirt that I'm convinced must
have been worn by Nicolas Sarkozy.

Not urinating in street

Urinating in street

MULTI-TASKING

Multi-tasking: it's easy. I'm listening to next door's dog barking (he's saying 'My owner isn't home yet. Please use your spare key and give me a walk'), while reading *Revolution in the Head*, while eating a biscuit and having a cup of tea, while watching *Star Wars II* with the boys, counting my musical instruments and wondering what I'm doing with my life.

bubblewrap

TWO-FOOT ROLL
OF BUBBLEWRAP

I was in my favourite stationery shop in all of
London, Fish & Cook on Blackstock Road, to
buy some of those horrible ink cartridges for my
printer. I was halfway home before I realised that
my two-year-old son had managed to nick a two-
foot roll of bubblewrap (he'd managed to conceal
it under his pram). We took it home and I phoned
The Stationer. He said he wouldn't get the police
involved this time, which was very gracious of him.
The two-foot roll of bubblewrap was immensely
versatile and the kids loved using it as a chunky light
sabre/intercontinental ballistic missile/head rest. I
now wish I'd kept the two-foot roll of bubblewrap.

I've a mate who used to have a bubblewrap fetish
(I don't really want to say any more). I don't love it
quite that much, but it's still amazing stuff.

THE METAPHOR PARROT

I was striding through the park one sunny afternoon when, out of the corner of my eye, I thought I spied a green parrot flitting between the treetops. I stopped to get a proper look, presuming I must have been mistaken. But there it was again. Flying now almost directly above me towards a large lime tree (OK, so I'm lying, I've no bloody idea what kind of tree it was) then disappearing into the mass of leaves. He looked completely out of place, like something from a children's picture book — *The Adventures of Green Parrot in North London*, or something like that. I decided that I had imagined the green parrot (I do read too many kids' books, it's true) and that the bird was simply a metaphor parrot, representing freedom, rebellion and individualism. I thanked my subconscious mind for the image, then carried on my journey to John's Garden Centre to buy some fish food.

However, a few weeks later, on our way back from swimming lessons, my kids saw the green parrot too. So he is actually merely an escaped parrot who is stuck in a cold North London park. Now we can't go through the park without our youngest spending ages under the trees shouting, 'Green parrot! Green parrot!'

Though apparently it's a parakeet.

Green

tastes lemony & grows too quickly

PLANTS I DON'T KNOW THE NAME OF: BITTER LETTUCEY STUFF

I bought this herb at the garden centre. It looked so unassuming and also quite healthy. I could add it to stews or salads, said the blurb on the back of the plastic tab that I've now lost, or possibly one of my boys is using it as a bookmark. But very soon the little green herb grew into a mass of huge leaves which seemed to grow at an alarming rate every day.

I once hacked away at some of the leaves – which seemed to grow back instantly – and added them to a stir fry. They tasted vinegary and bitter – in fact, it was just like eating leaves. My wife didn't notice.

RAPID E15 STAPLER

This 35cm-long stapler is a real boon for people like me who run a thriving and news-packed community newsletter. It allows you to staple in the middle of an A4 magazine and, if I were a different person, I'd say it was one of the most valuable items in my expanding stationery cupboard. Sadly, my thriving and news-packed community newsletter doesn't actually exist — it is something from that parallel universe in which I am a highly organised and motivated person. Instead my Rapid E15 stapler gets used for things like making space rockets out of toilet roll, or as a ruler, or a baseball bat, or a ramp for 1:72 scale soldiers (Italian Alpini regiment) to storm the enemy Care Bear/ Power Ranger Alliance stronghold on the arm of the sofa.

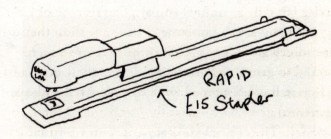

RAPID
E15 Stapler

CYRILLE KILLER

One of the kids has broken my treasured Subbuteo
Cyrille Regis. I don't have all that many sacred items
in my house . . . OK, I have loads — cupboards,
boxes and shelves crammed with them — but this
is the only one related to West Bromwich Albion,
and so I was pretty upset. I had to superglue his
ankles (Cyrille's, not my son's). The rest of the
1979 WBA team are missing. I have a feeling that
they took part in a big Airfix model recreation of
the D-Day landings some time in the early 80s (and
were possibly kidnapped by 1:72 scale Afrika Korps
figurines).

Cyrille lives on my desk now, a reminder that I
have never been able to paint small fiddly details and
that Ron Greenwood was over-cautious at the 1982
World Cup.

PLANTS I DON'T KNOW THE NAME OF: SOME HERB SEEDS I SCATTERED AROUND THE PLACE

A few years ago I read a book about medieval herbalism and, as I am wont to do, decided to make it a part of my life. I could be a herbalist! So I sent off for a load of seeds from a specialist shop and when they came, rather than sticking them in a drawer like I usually do, I scattered them all over the garden. All kinds of different seeds. Over the years various plants have come and gone but one seems to thrive but I don't know what it is. It's either Crimson Parsley, Herb Robert or Feverfew. Or a mixture of all three. The problem I have now is that, whereas Parsley is good for cooking, and Herb Robert is OK, Feverfew is, I think, poisonous. This is complicated further by the fact that there is no such thing as Crimson Parsley.

I've got be honest. I would be a really shit herbalist.

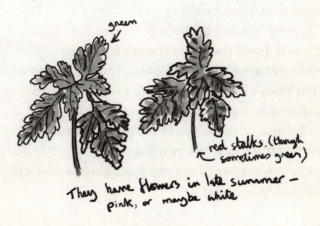

green

red stalks. (though sometimes green)

They have flowers in late summer – pink, or maybe white

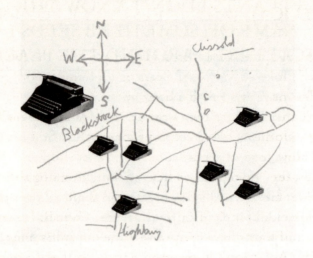

LOCAL WRITING HOTSPOTS

1. The writing tree in Clissold Park – an ancient horse chestnut on a little mound in the south-west corner of the park
2. Genesis Cafe on Blackstock Road (fast wireless internet and good coffee)
3. The no. 29 bus between Finsbury Park and Camden Town (but only if you get a seat)
4. The table near the window in that little cafe whose name I can't remember on the corner of Lordship Road and Stoke Newington Church Street
5. The cafe of the Clissold Leisure Centre. Though not the tables near the counter.
6. The front seats of the 141 bus between Clissold Park and Old Street.

LOCAL WILDLIFE: DIRTY FOXES

Walking home along Riversdale Road I see the tall
Irish bloke who's always cleaning and painting
his front yard. He's standing in the road looking
forlorn. As I get closer I can see rubbish – papers,
bags, clothes – strewn all over the place.

'How are you?' I say.

'Foxes.' he replies. 'They can smell the dog shit.
What a mess.'

I decide to help him clear up the rubbish. It's in
front of his house and he's very proud of his place, I
know. As if reading my mind he says, 'I like tidiness.
I hate mess like this.'

I find a brown shoe. 'It was a stylish one-legged
fox,' I say. He laughs. I find a copy of *Marie Claire*. 'It
was a stylish one-legged fox who is into fashion and
make-up tips.' He laughs again.

I see him later in the day and he waves. He is once
more cleaning his front yard.

TRAPPED

I have spent most of my London life a fundamentalist walker. I don't like to use the car too much. But every now and then I have to take a quick spin and today I took a short cut down a little back street and became trapped between a recycling truck and a breakdown lorry. I could feel the rage bubbling up inside me. Basically, I was trapped. Time seemed to slow down. The refuse collectors kept dropping bottles on the road, which would smash and then they'd spend an age clearing it up. It was like a Damien Hirst installation called The Frustration Of Being Trapped Within The Confines Of Time, Space And A Recycling Lorry When You Need To Get Somewhere In A Hurry.

There was a flurry of excitement when it looked like they had cleared the stretch of recycling boxes, then – SMASH! – another couple of bottles hit the deck. I had to grab myself around the neck to stop me rushing into the street and screaming at them. Luckily I found an *A-Z* in the car and tricked myself into calming down by flicking through it.

HANGOVERS

I've had some beautiful hangovers since moving to this part of North London in the late 90s but nothing that compares with the body-numbing trips of old where I'd have to sit in a park and stare at the sky for hours. But they would still come now and then and I would welcome them like old friends. Sometimes I used to sit on the top deck of a bus and try to trick the hangover by changing buses and getting on another one. (But hangovers are smart and they soon got wise to that one.)

I cherished these hangovers as they happened so infrequently. To be honest, they were more like old annoying friends who'd come to stay for the day when you had loads of things you needed to do. Then one year I got a worse than usual hangover, from drinking German lager (which I rarely do), and the next day was the holidays and I was minding the children. I got cross with the hangover and after that the hangovers stopped coming to stay.

BIKE CHAINS AND FENG SHUI

On my road today one of my neighbours was trying
to put the chain back on her bike.

'Her chain's bust,' shouted the tall Irish bloke
from across the road, out tending his front garden.

I stopped to help. The bike wasn't in good nick
and I couldn't get the chain to work. The Irish bloke
came over and we started discussing how this part of
the road might be haunted, as my hands got more
and more covered in oil.

'It's bad feng shui,' said the tall Irish bloke. 'All
the chi is flowing off down Wyatt Road. That's why
I'm poor,' he laughed, pointing at his jumper full of
holes. I told them about the New River which used
to flow under their houses and we started discussing
plans to reinstate a stretch of it on Riversdale Road.

'Did you know there was a battle between the Danes
and the Saxons round here?' said the Irish bloke.

I said I did, though I can't remember how I found
it out — perhaps on a rainy afternoon in Guildhall
Library from an obscure book whose title I wrote down
in a now lost notebook. The area was once known as
Danebottom, a reminder of a group of Scandinavian
lads who came over for a European away tie and never
went home. We discussed the possibility that the road
might be haunted by the ghost of a Viking, then the
tall Irish bloke realised he hadn't done any front yard
tidying for at least fifteen minutes, and scooted off
home.

Charlie George →

Peter Lorimer ↗

TRADITIONAL CRAFTS - FOOTBALL ARM TATTOOS

Not so long ago I was asked to man the face-painting stall at the school fete. 'You draw pictures,' they said. 'You'll be great.' What could go wrong? In fact I was the worst face-painter the world has ever seen — my 'butterflies' looked like masks made of sick. If only I'd thought of squashed butterflies — I might have got more of the boys interested. So the next year I improvised and offered footballer arm tattoos.

It's now my official profession. (Well, one of them at any rate.)

NEWINGTON GREEN

A fancy neighbourhood for progressive types since the 1600s. In fact the oldest terraced houses in London (1658) are on the square. Daniel Defoe lived here, as did Mary Wollstonecraft and John Stuart Mill. It's home to the Unitarian Chapel, the China Inland Mission, the Mildmay Club and a nice kids' cafe. From here roads take you quickly to Stoke Newington, Islingon, Haringay, Highbury and the distant rehearsal studios of Dalston.

CAFE REVIEWS
N19 CAFE, HOLLOWAY ROAD

I came in the early evening and sat down with
my strong little cup of coffee to watch the sea of
humanity on Holloway Road flow by – families,
workers, couples, old folk, kids, joggers, bikes, cars,
lorries, buses. Lavazza Americano is served in a little
white enamel cup. Midge Ure on the radio and he's
actually quite interesting, talking about how he got
to become the singer in Ultravox but inevitably all
the presenter wants to know about is Bob Geldof and
Live Aid. The melancholy-eyed woman sweeping up
is half listening to it, then a bloke comes in and says
it's time to shut up now. So I go a bit further down
the road, about 100 yards, for a similar coffee where
80s power ballads are blaring out and at a nearby
table a young woman is talking very loudly about her
girlfriend and travel escapades and how she could
never have sex with a bloke. 'Urgh, the thought!' she
says, as her quiet friend tries to calm her agitated
baby.

GOODBYE FOOTBALL TREE

A while ago (I can't remember — was it three years or six months?) a spherical wicker sculpture was placed on top of the remains of one of the old trees that had died after the 2003 drought. It seemed to be saying that the tree could continue to have a life after it had died.

Every day my youngest son and I walk through Clissold Park and go up to touch the Football Tree.

'Football Tree!' my son will say. We'll then both have a quiet think about how great football and trees are, and walk on.

But the Football Tree is no more. The other morning as we approached it as part of our daily pilgrimage, we saw the wicker sphere lying smashed on the ground. Next to it was an iron pole, part of a nearby fairground display. Still fresh in the air was the sense that someone had decided that good stuff was rubbish and had to be ruined. Was this part of the artist's planned trajectory for the sculpture — to hire a gang of bored and drunk idiots to destroy it?

My son said he wanted to fix the football tree. I told him that it couldn't be fixed because it was a metaphor for the world's problems. Or the problems of bored and drunk idiots hanging around in parks at night. Or the England football team's problems. Or the problems of sentimentalising outdoor installation sculpture.

The raspberries that moved from next door

LOCAL WILDLIFE: RASPBERRIES

When we first moved into the house at the start of 1999, the old lady next door used to leave us little trays of raspberries on the wall. She was in her mid-70s and had been born and brought up in the area around our street. This carried on for two or three years until around 2003, when I first started doing a bit of gardening and, as if at the behest of some benign gardening spirit, her raspberries went under the garden wall into our garden.

For years we had a great crop, but after a while they began to dominate one whole side of the (not very big) plot and for the amount of foliage there wasn't really that much fruit. However, the kids would certainly disagree. They love picking raspberries before breakfast or for their pudding.

In the end I had to pull up most of the raspberries. I've left a few plants, for the kids' pre-breakfast snack and as a reminder of Edna's little acts of kindness.

LONDON PLACES THAT I REALLY LIKE — HOBGOBLIN

A NICE LONDON PLACE: HOBGOBLIN

One of my favourite walks into the West End takes me to Rathbone Street, where the Hobgoblin music shop is situated. The trouble with shops like this is that I always want to buy something, usually an obscure instrument that I can't afford, like a harp, dulcimer, or banjo-mandolin. After scouting around various shops in London for a mandolin for my new Irish music class, I eventually take my old Eko 12-string guitar here and basically swap it for a cheap but easy to play Blue Moon mandolin. The blokes at Hobgoblin are quite an amusing duo. One is a quickfire comedy powerhouse. The other is quiet and intense.

Not long after that I saw the film *Juno*, and at the end Paulie Bleeker, the gawky character played by Michael Cera, plays the guitar with Juno and it's an old Eko 12-string. Has he just bought my old guitar? I have a pang of regret at the sight of it. But after a few deep breaths I decide I'm happy with the mandolin and it's sort of changed my life in the sense that for the first time in many years I've been actively learning something and it doesn't matter that I'm not that good at it.

The bloke in 'Juno' with my guitar

I KNOW A PATH WHERE
THE COW PARSLEY GROWS

This is cow parsley that I found on Parkland Walk, the track along the old railway line from Finsbury Park to Highgate. Although it's slightly cack-handed flower drawing I also like to think that in some way it is a portrait of a world-view — that the seemingly mundane can be beautiful.

TWO METAPHOR
PARROTS ARE COMPANY...

Strolling through the park from the Stoke
Newington end I look up and see the Green
Metaphor Parrot — with a girlfriend. They are
perched on a branch, kissing. Then they fly to
another bit of the tree and cuddle up together. Of
course, I have no way of knowing that my Metaphor
Parrot is male. But I feel happy for him/her.

This is all exciting enough. But further down the
tree is a huge great green (metaphor) parrot/parakeet
with its head in a hole, seemingly sucking the life
force out of the tree — or possibly the whole park —
like something out of *Doctor Who*.

I look around. People are walking past completely
oblivious to what is going on above their heads. No
one else is staring at the tree or wondering when our
Alien Parrot Life Force-Draining And Smooching
Parrot/Parakeet Overlords will take over Stoke
Newington completely. It appears no one else can see
them except me and my kids. It's a gift we must use
wisely for the good of mankind.

TALKING WITH THE DOG PEOPLE

While the numbers of Dog People frequenting Clissold Park has grown enormously over the past few years, one of the things that hasn't changed is their inability to see normal humans. I have always been able to walk amongst them, seemingly invisible, without so much as a glance. I could have marched into the middle of a group of them and emptied a bag of Winalot on their heads and they wouldn't have noticed.

This week, because our neighbour is poorly, I've been walking her dog most days. (Breed? Er, it's a little brown dog that looks uncannily like Robin Smith, the late Labour MP.) Today we ventured into the park. I wasn't in twenty seconds when two Dog People approached me, smiling in a strange friendly way.

'Hello!' one of them said. Was she talking to me? I must have looked startled.

'He looks like he needs a good run!' beamed her friend.

'Aren't you going to let him off his lead?'

'He's very friendly!'

Their eye contact was unbearably intense. I didn't dare let him run free yet, I said. But if I let go of the lead perhaps I would become invisible to the Dog People once more. Most likely the effects of the dog wear off over time. Luckily I was pushing a pram with the other hand and my son was able to get me out of danger by crying.

LOCAL WILDLIFE: THE LIQUORICE TREE

Between two smallish trees in Clissold Park there is a long length of red twine that somebody (conceptual nature artist or mischievous kitten) has wrapped round and round many times. It's saying, 'We are connected in ways that we don't fully understand.' It's also saying, 'Imagine a world where red liquorice grows from the trees. Yum!' It might also be an advert for the wool shop on Blackstock Road. Or perhaps it's saying, 'Look how fragile is existence' or 'Look how fragile is the Arsenal back four when a ball is played over the top.'

LONDON CALLING

Seemingly out of the blue, my friend Lee asked me
yesterday if I knew that The Clash had recorded
the *London Calling* album in Highbury. It's the kind of
anal-retentive conversational nugget I usually love
to hoard away for a rainy day but on this occasion
I was out-anal-retentived. Apparently it was at
Wessex Studios, at the old church on Highbury New
Park. Maybe it's St Augustine's. When quizzed, Lee
admitted he'd seen an article about it in the *Independent*
a few weeks ago.

What Lee didn't tell me, and what I had to
find out myself at the University of The Clash's
history archive, was that the song 'Rudie Can't Fail'
specifically mentions Blackstock Road's bus, the
number 19.

When Joe Strummer died I went down to the
old record shop in Stoke Newington and re-bought
vinyl copies of *Give 'Em Enough Rope* and *London Calling*. (I'd
flogged my originals to one of my brothers many
years earlier.)

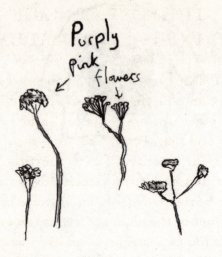

Purply
pink
flowers

PLANTS I DON'T KNOW THE
NAME OF: PURPLY PINK FLOWERS

At the far end of the park there is a raised bed with
clusters of tall pinky purple flowers on long slender
stems that appeared in one of the smaller park
redesigns a few years ago. I've always been fascinated
by them. There's something mesmerising about the
way they sway in a gentle breeze. I think it might be
Valerian. I've been suffering from mild insomnia for
the past couple of years — something I used to get as
a kid — and wonder whether a harvest of these flowers
might help me (though if I did that I'm sure I'd find
out they're something completely different).

THE LOST STORAGE CONTAINER OF COLDFALL WOOD

On one of my longer-distance jaunts into the mysterious lands beyond Muswell Hill, I discover a large blue steel storage container at the edge of Coldfall Wood. Something about it — the slightly open door, the incongruity of its functional insignia (AFRO written in big white letters) suggests it might be a portal to the parallel universe I am often seeking. (I sense that sometimes I respond to urban life with a kind of hungry, imaginative escapism.)

But I don't venture into the new world of the storage container — I come back through Muswell Hill and Crouch End, then get the W7 bus down to Finsbury Park. Of course, the storage container no longer stands near the wood. It must be hidden away in some obscure storage facility in the outer London industrial zone, waiting for someone else to find it.

not really
crooked — I can't
draw straight
lines

COLOURED FINE LINER PENS

At the stationers on Blackstock Road I buy three fine liner pens – pink, purple and green.

'Strange colour scheme, there,' says the stationer. He often feels the need to comment on my purchases.

'Doing notes and referencing,' I say.

'In purple?'

I want to say to him: 'Why do you have purple pens if you are uncomfortable about people buying them?' But I just smile.

The coloured pens are actually a trap to prove that my kids are always stealing my fine liner pens, but that is too complicated to explain.

THE REAL PSYCHIC GENIUS
FOOTBALL PREDICTION SOCIETY

If you are a regular visitor to the public houses of
North London you might have noticed a group of
forty- and fifty-something men and women loudly
discussing football and politics while brandishing
spreadsheets and graphs and drinking a little too
quickly. Chances are you have stumbled upon the
legendary Real Psychic Genius Football Prediction
Society. Their supposed aims are to guess as near as
possible the final placings of the English Premier
League. However, they are rubbish at staying on
topic. They are as much a part of the old pubs they
frequent as the lovely glasswork, high ornate ceilings
and fine wood bars.

In some ways they are what search engines were
like before the internet was invented. Ask them
something and they will all have an answer (actually,
an opinion) and will spend the next twenty minutes
arguing about who is right.

The Real Psychic Genius
Football Prediction Society

THE NORTH LONDON COMPENDIUM OF LOST THINGS: MY GRANDFATHER'S RETIREMENT WATCH

This is all a bit like that memory game where you try to recall an object that has been taken away. Sometimes you only notice that object after it's gone. When the ball is in a group of other toys the child won't see it. But when there is a ball-shaped gap the kid will shout 'Ball!'

So it is with my Grandfather's retirement watch. I was finally given my Grandfather's retirement watch in 1987, five years after he died. My mum and my gran decided that I was ready, responsible enough

to look after it. And I was. I hid it at the back of a drawer in my room of the house I shared with friends in Walthamstow. I'd only wear it on special occasions, like a job interview or going for a beer. But during one of our break-ins in 1989 it was stolen. I never really thought about my Grandfather's retirement watch when I had it but now, over twenty years on, I still think about it all the time. Every time I pass an antique shop or stall, anything with old watches, I stop and have to check that my Grandfather's watch isn't among them.

'To Frank Sowden. For 50 years' service, on your retirement from Anderton's Mill, Cleckheaton.

Don't give it to your feckless grandson. He'll only lose it.'

I should
have ordered
the soup

PLANTS I DON'T KNOW THE NAME OF: HAD THEM IN A RESTAURANT IN ISLINGTON

I ordered these years ago, not knowing what they were. This ball of barky leaf came back. I complained to the waiter (it was a French restaurant) that the dish wasn't cooked properly. He sort of sneered as if to say, 'Sir doesn't go to restaurants very often, does Sir?'

I had them years later in Brittany. One of the signature dishes in the little town we stayed in, not far from Roscoff, was a plate of artichoke leaves and a bottle of cider. I can see how, traditionally, the cider worked. It masked the metaphysical pain that the Bretons felt at the knowledge that their most famous meal was a pile of tasteless barky leaves.

1st Wld War tank.

Drawing of World War One Tank at the Imperial War Museum While Waiting for the Kids to Come Back from the Loo

TAKE ME TO TOMATO PARADISE

I had a dream in which I lived in the countryside in a tomato paradise. All kinds of different plants grew, all with huge tasty fruit, including a whole row of different kinds of plum tomatoes which looked more like giant peppers. Various friends were there, too, enjoying the tasty tomatoes. I finished one which had an ash tree seed in it and planted it by an old metal sink that was plonked down in another part of the garden.

But the problem with enjoying a dream garden too much is that you start to neglect your real garden. It feels too wet and miserable — it's small and bedraggled and at the moment unloved (by me at any rate). It just reminds me of chores. Things that have to be done. I look at the holes in the fence, the weeds, the mud, the bare grass, the old dustbin filled with plastic toys. I need to get my garden shit* together.

* Obviously I don't mean manure. I mean my motivation for doing odd-jobs.

FADING LEAVES

Yet another of the old horse chestnut trees in Clissold Park is starting to peg out. On the south side, near the route of the buried New River, this tree always dominated that section of the park. Now, though, while the sides of the tree are still verdant and healthy, the whole middle part appears to be dying — the leaves are thin or non-existent. It looks like it's had a monk's haircut. It's a Ralph Coates tree — actually, a Terry Mancini tree would be a more accurate description. Was it something to do with the fair, which visits two or three times a year and always in the same spot? Perhaps some of the chemicals used in the candy floss-making process have been leaching into the soil? Or is it connected to the groundwater problems in this bit of the park? The ranger said that he had wondered about the fair (though not the candy floss connection).

Some of the other old trees in the park are being cut down. A few of the gnarled horse chestnut trees in the south-west corner have seemingly died in the last year and spent the summer without leaves. Now they wear an X and wait for the chainsaw. Two came down last week and another three will soon follow. One of them has purple rings tied around various branches, presumably in some kind of North London tribute to the 70s song 'Tie a Yellow Ribbon Round the Old Oak Tree'.

CAFE WITH ART
BLAKEY CD PLAYING,
MORNINGTON CRESCENT

I went in for a chicken and avocado toasted sandwich
and a coffee at a little cafe opposite the station. As
soon as I sat down Talk Radio was turned off and
what sounded like Art Blakey and the Jazz Messengers
came blaring out of the speakers. A middle-aged
man comes in and tries to get pally with the bloke
behind the counter.

– So, you Italian?

– No.

– Maltese?

– No.

– Iranian?

– No.

There's a brief silence. The older man looks
around.

– So you do food?

His new mate looks around him at the sandwiches
and salads on display and arches an eyebrow.

My toasted sandwich is still very hot. In a
pedestrian island in the middle of the road I can see
a statue of the anti-Corn Law campaigner Richard
Cobden. The Corn Laws were a vital part of my 19th
century British history module at A-Level, but I
failed to concentrate in lessons due to the presence
of a very pretty and very young substitute teacher

who had just arrived from teacher training college. When it came to the exam a few months later and the relevant question, all I could think of was her face, smiling and blinking in slow motion, as she says something about Peel and free trade.

There wasn't much avocado in it.

STATUE
← of Cobden

THE NECK OF MY GUITAR AS
SEEN THROUGH A HEAT HAZE

I'm testing out my eyesight this afternoon and I still
can't see straight lines. I try out my wang eye (the
left) on my guitar and the neck shimmers and breaks
up at the edges, as if looked at from a distance in
a heat haze. Everything is thinner, too, especially
people's faces. If I try to read through my left eye
only, it's as if publishing has been taken over by
incompetent typesetters.

HOLLOWAY ROAD

It's the start of the A1, the road to the north (and the western edge of my village). Over the years it's had a bad reputation but you can still see that in the 19th century it must have been a fashionable shopping boulevard. Holloway Road is still the place to come for dodgy second-hand electronic gear, black market tobacco and (further north) old men's pubs.

SOME LOVELY THINGS
ON THE KINGSLAND ROAD

Walking around aimlessly a bit further east than
usual, I find a fantastic market on the peeled and
faded long-gone glamour of Kingsland Road, where
history hasn't yet been cleaned off the bricks, the
streets and the paintwork. In the low bright sunlight
of the broad boulevard there are lots of little stalls
with some niche product lines.

One stall has just a toaster and an opened can
of Skol Super. The next has an old record player, a
pair of gloves and a battered copy of *War and Peace*. His
neighbour is offering three pairs of shoes, an old
A-Z and a Bush radio. Then it starts getting really
high-end – a little table with five different Ben Elton
books (the one about the funny bloke and that one
about Australia and the other one and the one about
a bloke and a girl) and some miscellaneous jewellery.

Then, just before things start getting a bit boringly
orthodox with the hardware, clothes and shoe stalls,
I find the stall I've been looking for all my life. All
it has is a plastic toy car, a drill and a couple of old
78s. At times like this I could almost fall in love with
capitalism.

RETURN OF THE MICE

Having been away in Ireland for two weeks, we got
home to find the mice have returned and the piano
is de-tuned. There must be a connection. But I am
tired of wrestling with the thought of killing mice.
Why can't we live together in harmony? After all, the
mice aren't asking for much – all they want is cheese,
nuts and a nice clean surface to poo on.

BLACKBERRY WAY

A Hackney Brook walk around to the new Arsenal
stadium to gawp at some concrete and cranes, then a
quick sketching session (still can't draw blackberries)
in Gillespie Park with my Dad. Actually, I didn't
know blackberries lasted so long into the autumn.

The wetlands are dry, due to a leak caused no doubt
by scuba diving vandals with harpoon guns, and part
of the parkland is closed up for renovations. If only
London could have more strange wild areas like this.
Perhaps the mayor could pull down a couple of glass
and concrete monsters in the City and create a new
London International Centre for Blackberry Studies.

'Algernon, coming to the champers bar for lunch?'

'No ta, chum, I'm off blackberry picking so auntie
can make some jam for tea!'

THE RED-FACED BLOKE
DOG SHIT INCIDENT

The bloke was in his early 20s and had a stripy T-shirt and a spotty red face. He swaggered out of the King's Head with his dog then watched, transfixed, as the dog did a big runny shit all over the pavement. He was about to swagger off in the direction of Finsbury Park when I told him if everyone acted like that the world would be covered in dog shit. He looked at me in disbelief. 'How will I clear it up?' he whined. I pointed to the paper bag he was holding, which contained a brand new tube of what I presume was acne cream. The dog looked up at his master as if to say, 'Want me to bite his gonads?' but the bloke still seemed confused, as if he had never realised that leaving dog shit on the pavement was wrong. I left him standing, baffled, over the pile of crap.

My daughter said that as soon as my back was turned he swaggered over to the bus stop as if nothing had happened.

AUTUMN

(Sad but somehow
satisfying)

bills → rubber bands ←

POSTMAN PATTER

Bright sunshine and cold breezes this morning, as befits the first official day of autumn. The postman says there are no letters for us today but that we can have some rubber bands.

'What for?' I ask.

'For the kids. So they can make, er, space rockets and stuff.'

He roots around in his postman wheelie trolley and fishes out a large handful of big thick brown rubber bands.

'Do you have any used toilet rolls as well, then?'

'What for?'

'Well, to make the rockets.'

He smiles and sticks up a thumb. 'Arsenal!' he says, non-sequiturially, and starts to walk up the hill.

A COLD WIND BLOWS
FROM WOODBERRY DOWN

It's the same every morning. At the end of the tree-lined bank that used to carry the New River, as you turn vaguely northwards towards the fenced-off no-dogs area, the temperature all of a sudden drops. A cold dry wind hits your face, whirling in from the direction of Woodberry Down. Narrow your eyes and you can see that you're on the slopes of a very gentle hill.

A can of Kestrel Super lies at the side of the path. A possible sign that a shamanic special brew energy diviner has been in the area, mapping the lines between Stoke Newington and Highbury. That or a lazy drunk.

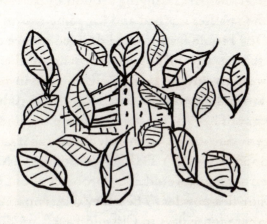

THE DOG People
(They like to bark
And they live in the park)

RETURN OF THE DOG PEOPLE

The Dog People of Clissold Park have been growing in number since the end of the summer. Now they are all over the park, hanging around in factions. Today the weather was bad and for some reason two of the Dog People factions had decided to face off on the footpath at the north-east corner of the park. There were around 30 dogs in all, covered in mud, racing around happily. But the Dog People didn't look happy. They all just stared off into the mid-distance at the other Dog People faction as if to say, 'They don't know ANYTHING about dogs'. Now and then someone would chat, probably about dog biscuits or flea powder. Then they'd carry on staring.

These are tense days in Clissold Park.

QUINK (BLACK)

'Do you sell Quink?' I said to my local stationer.

'Do we sell Quink? Of course we sell Quink. That's a strange question.'

'Well, it's the digital age. I wasn't sure that people still used Quink.' He snorts with derision and sells me the Quink, while also slipping in some crafty cross-selling and getting me to buy two expensive black ink cartridges for my inkjet printer.

I used to do loads of stuff in Quink, until I bought myself a Wacom art pad in 1997. There was a girl I worked with when I first came to London who drew wild landscapes in Quink. I fancied her, of course, but she had an on-off relationship with a Scottish rugby player so I didn't get involved. He didn't play for Scotland or anything, he was just Scottish and played rugby. We lost touch around 1989 but I kept her memory alive by starting to draw my own pictures in Quink. My pictures weren't wild, mostly just sketches of fat people at Walthamstow market or caricatures of my flatmates.

I KILLED THE CHERRY TREE

I bought two dwarf cherry trees and gave one to a friend whose father had recently died, as a sort of... I don't know what really. I planted the other one in a corner of our garden. The friend's tree thrived and budded, leafed and blossomed. Our tree grew some weedy leaves then seemed to stop. People would come round and look at the tree and remark that it seemed to be in the wrong place. Getting a bit angry with the tree and myself, I dug it up and moved it to a sunnier position near the raspberries. The tree faltered. Its leaves started to go brown. I watched the tree daily but it seemed to be doing worse there. So I dug it up a second time and put it in a big pot. This seemed to finish the tree off. All the leaves fell off and soon it was gone. The little branches snapped off easily, there was no life in it.

I think I've just lived through one of Aesop's fables.

THE WOOD COLLECTOR

Once a year our neighbour cuts back his apple tree then uses a big shredder (like in the Coen Brothers' *Fargo*). Once he asked if I'd like some wood for my barbeque. I said yes. Now he always saves me several bags full. Fantastic, I grin, lying through my teeth. For years I stored all the bags in the old outside toilet where he can't see them, then they built a new recycling centre over in Holloway and I took them all away.

The front trees and hedges we cut together. He has the equipment and the know-how and I clear it all up. Recently I spent ages collecting up lovely straight sticks then tying them together in neat bundles like something from a Thomas Hardy novel. Then I took them down the recycling centre and chucked them in a huge skip. It's what the Mayor of Casterbridge would have done.

old
cafe
at
King's
Cross

JAZZ
record
shop

This was always my favourite building in King's
Cross. It's got a strange lighthouse thing on the roof,
to help late-night revellers find their way back home,
I suppose. There used to be a little coffee place in
the left-hand stretch which I was always reminded
of whenever I heard 'Mario's Cafe' by St Etienne.
Behind it is the Scala where I used to go to all-night
B-movie film screenings (now I go there to see
bluegrass bands).

READING GLASSES

Went to the optician the other day, after losing yet
another pair of glasses in a messing-about-with-the-
kids incident.

'Your eyesight is maturing,' said the optician.

'What, you mean I appreciate art and ballet a bit
more now and fancy Fay Weldon?'

'Er, no, you need reading glasses.'

'Hmm. So I'm not short sighted any more?'

'You're still short sighted. You'll still need
distance lenses as well.'

In other words, there is only a depth of field of
about three inches in which my vision is clear.

I am shagged.

M Y E Y

E S A R E C

O M P L E T E L Y

S H A G G E D . B U

G G E R I T!

REPLICA KIT HEARTBREAK

It's non-uniform 'wear your football kit' day at my kids' school tomorrow and my oldest boy (seven) has decided that he no longer wants to wear Dublin or Clare GAA colours, but an English football team shirt. He has always said he supports Leeds so I said I'd be happy to sort him out.

'No, Dad, I want an Arsenal shirt.'

'But. But what about Leeds?'

'Arsenal.'

(My voice getting high-pitched and whiny) 'You said you supported Leeds.'

'They're all right. But I want an Arsenal shirt.'

'Eddie Gray . . . er, Arthur Graham . . . Ken Bates?'

He doesn't understand.

'Arsenal.'

'Look, I'm happy for you to *like* your local village team — which just happens to be Arsenal — but you need a big northern team too.' He shakes his head. 'All my friends support Arsenal.'

So this morning I trudged down the road to the Arsenal shop. Now that two of my children have become Gooners I only have one kid left — my three-year-old — to indoctrinate with my irrational, heartbreaking and futile love of Leeds United.

I might have to resort to bribes with this one.

ARSENAL v PORTSMOUTH (MATCH REPORT)

Winter is closing in. The tits in our back garden have almost run out of nuts and the mice are so starving they've taken to eating from the box of mouse poison that's been in the cupboard under the sink for the last year. It always gets cold in the days just after Christmas. Which is why I haven't left the house all day.

A friend phoned and asked if I was doing anything tonight.

'No,' I said.

'Fancy going to see Arsenal v Portsmouth?'

'No,' I said.

'Er, OK then. Bye.'

Instead I cracked open some beers and watched telly with my wife. There was one chocolate left from the really fancy box and I said she could have it.

MOSTLY PINK (sometimes blue)

We have loads of these.

PLANTS I DON'T KNOW THE NAME OF*: BIG OLD LADY FLOWERS FROM ANOTHER ERA

These big-headed plants dominated our garden for years. For a few brief seconds — OK, a few days at most — they would be topped by big fluffy insipidly pink flowers (or sometimes blue) which would then dry out very quickly and sit there for months as if to say, 'What shall I do now?' These plants were like some sort of old-fashioned technology that no longer has relevance in the 21st century. We have two of these plants at the side return next to our kitchen, but their days are numbered. Soon work will start on a kitchen extension, a project developed solely for the purpose of getting rid of them.

* Yes, I now know they're hydrangeas. Put down your book of Old Lady Garden Flowers.

NICE VIEW OF 19TH-CENTURY GAS HOLDERS (THE LINCOLN LOUNGE, YORK WAY)

If the definition of a good pub is a solid pint, battered old seats, some books lying about, a view out the window of a 19th-century gas holder and a hardworking yet bewitching Irish barmaid then the Lincoln Lounge is most certainly a good pub. Situated in the shifting atmosphere of the greater King's Cross urban zone, The Lincoln Lounge is a late Victorian old men's pub done up for the new old men of the early 21st century. And if it's not too busy then your not-too-cold Guinness will be brought to you on a tray by the resident high-booted Irish goth barvixen. Nice 30s-style mural on the back wall too.

LOCAL WILDLIFE: LONDON BIRDS

I had to stop and listen to the massed tree-top bird orchestra in Clissold Park this evening. It sounded like the echoing cacophony of a rainforest, except with added police sirens, trundling buses, car horns, people shouting. I wish I could be more specific and say it was a flock of starlings preparing to head off for Eastern Africa or a shedload of blackbirds having a sing-off. Or even some crafty magpies with a stolen (battery powered) echo chamber. But, sadly, I never properly perused the *Eye Spy Book of Birds* that my Uncle Kenneth bought me for Christmas when I was ten.

FOX NEWS: THREE FOXES IN SEARCH OF A HALF-EATEN PIZZA

I was working late when I heard a commotion outside – it sounded like someone trying to kick over a compost bin. Expecting to see some alcopopped adolescents expressing their distaste for conformist society, I instead caught sight of three foxes sprinting away. They then had a sniff around the bins of number 55 across the road before one of them made that strange foxy yelp-bark and off they ran towards the park.

I wanted to shout out to them, 'You're wasting your time. They're all vegetarians in Stoke Newington.' But it was very late. And I don't speak foxy yelp-bark.

THE URBAN COUNTRY PROJECT

Great news for local music fans. My band, Magic Orange, has reformed, except there are now only two of us. The lead guitarist lives in Switzerland. The drummer has disappeared — though he used to tell me he wanted to run a chain of hotels, so he's probably in some tax-free island haven by now. And I married the backing singer. Now it's just me and my friend Doug, and we call ourselves The Urban Country Project (which in retrospect sounds a bit too town planning-ish for a band).

We usually rehearse down in Dalston, when childcare and other stuff allows. When I mention the group to people they laugh and say, 'Don't give up your day job.' I haven't had a day job for seventeen years, so I don't know what they're on about. Maybe I should get a job first, then I can jack it in when we go on tour.

Doug is a lean and watchful Ray Davies type. I'm more like a chunky Kris Kristofferson with lower back problems. I'm sure we are twice the age of most of the bands who practise there. And whereas they book it out for serious once-a-week sessions, ours tend to be three times a year, tops. Don't want to get stale.

The rehearsal studio bloke seems nice but he's a bit scatterbrained so sometimes he doesn't turn up and we are left standing outside. Those are the best nights. We hang around for a while in the cold and chat about our families, football, music, life, then go down the pub.

I'VE GOT WHEELS
AND A FULL TANK OF GAS

I've got wheels and a full tank of gas. To be more specific, it's a full tank of high-performance unleaded petrol. I drove out of the garage on Hornsey Road thinking to myself, 'I could go anywhere, do anything. Just drive and see where the road takes me.'

But rather than head up to Scotland to camp out in the hills I drove straight home and then spent 40 minutes looking at the *Star Wars* Lego website with the kids.

LEEDS UNITED v TOTTENHAM HOTSPUR (MATCH REPORT)

The Auld Shillelagh in Stoke Newington Church Street used to be my favourite pub in North London, but I haven't been in for a while. I must be getting old because the ruralesque walk around Clissold Park at night doesn't seem as appealing as it once did.

I was there with old friends from the Real Psychic Genius Football Prediction Society. The Shillelagh is really our spiritual home but we now tend to wander a bit down the road to the Rose & Crown, where the music isn't loud and there's lots of space for assorted fortysomethings to shuffle around slowly. Leeds v Spurs is on the telly. I pick a famously unlucky seat – where I had watched England lose to Brazil in the 2002 World Cup and from where I'd seen Ireland throw away the lead in the last minute in qualifiers countless times. It doesn't disappoint. Leeds lose. But the Guinness is as good as ever and there's still a good mix of old and young drinking away. One big change is last orders, which is now an orthodox 11-ish rather than at four in the morning. But I suppose that's progress. As my wife said when I rolled in, last orders was invented for people like me who need authority figures such as barmaids to tell them what to do.

OVERCOMING
WRITER'S BLOCK

On a 29 bus heading into Camden I look for some
paper in my pockets and get out an old receipt then
start to write on the back of it. The ideas come thick
and fast, but I have to write very small because it's
not a very big receipt. On a bus I'm freed from
expectation. I remember all the things that have been
lying around in my mind. I also recognise the things
I'm looking at rather than only half noticing them.
I don't have a computer screen in front of me and
I'm not listening to music. Just me, the pen, a small
receipt, and writing so tiny that actually I won't be
able to decipher any of it when I get home unless I
jot stuff down on my hand. But better out than in,
eh?

Tea Time at The Worker's Cafe, Holloway Road

existing building

ghost building

tree

NORTH LONDON COMPENDIUM OF LOST THINGS: THE CHURCH NEAR THE BENCH WITH THE NICE VIEW

My late neighbour, Edna, knew more about local history than anyone I know. One afternoon, as we chatted over the garden fence, she started to tell me about St John's church. I didn't know anything about this and she explained that it was demolished in the early 80s due to a shortage of modernist-looking flats in the area (or something like that).

This spot is one of my favourite parts of Highbury. When my daughter started school at the top of the hill I'd sit on the bench on the other side of the road from the missing church and look down into the vale and beyond, marvelling at the semi-rural template that lay beneath the concreted scene.

In some ways it doesn't matter so much that the church is no longer there. If I concentrate I can see it just as plainly as if it was there in front of me. In fact in a bizarre way I notice it more. It's the same with other parts of the village. If I sit on the viewing bench and imagine the scene without the buildings, imagine looking down over pastures and meadows with the New River winding its way through the landscape from Hornsey over towards Stoke Newington. And there, to the left of the scene, snaking down from the Crouch Hill heights to the west, is the Hackney Brook.

Perhaps realising that the modernist-looking flats/knock-down-the-church thing wasn't such a great idea after all, the council have erected a smart new bench so that people can look at the church that isn't there anymore. The bench is more comfortable than the old one but for some reason I'm less inclined to sit on it for very long. I tell myself that I should spend half a day sitting down at this spot watching life unfold around me and see the changing light over Finsbury Park as the afternoon unfurls. These days I tell myself I'm too busy to do this. Perhaps one day, soon.

THE RUGBY BABIES

It's a rain-dappled, chilly Sunday morning in
Clissold Park. Lots of little kids in blue jerseys are
running around on the wet boggy grass. I'm holding
a size 3 rugby ball and flicking it around in my
fingers, and send a pass out to the first of the kids.
He passes it straight back to me. I'm now in my fifth
year of coaching kids at Hackney Bulls youth rugby
club. I call my lot the rugby babies. They are all
between five and seven years old.

One of the other coaches walks over.

'Did you hear that thing on the radio about
Juliette Gréco? Superb!'

He then tells me all about Paris and the
existentialists.

He pauses, then – 'So, are your lads up for the
game against Chingford then?' he says.

It's the kind of question Sartre might have asked.

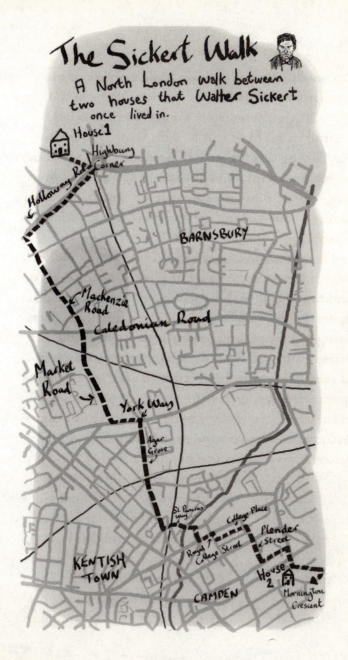

The Sickert Walk

A North London walk between two houses that Walter Sickert once lived in.

House 1

Highbury Corner

Holloway Rd

BARNSBURY

Mackenzie Road

Caledonian Road

Market Road →

York Way

Agar Grove

St Pancras Way

KENTISH TOWN

College Place

Royal College Street

Plender Street

House 2

Mornington Crescent

CAMDEN

THE ESSAY

I'm watching my oldest son write a review of his favourite book. He writes the title, then the author's name, then immediately his eyes start to swivel around in his head and he's thinking, 'Jesus I've been doing this for *ages*', so he starts drawing faces on his fingertips. A happy face, a sad face, a bored face. 'How do you do angry faces?' he asks. I explain to him about sloping the eyebrows down. 'Oh yeah. Thanks.'

He sees me watching him and goes back to his essay. He writes the name of the illustrator then sighs as if the weight of the world is on his shoulders. He draws one more face on his little finger then starts a finger puppet show, doing little high-pitched voices as they all chat to each other. After a couple of minutes I say to him, 'Homework?' and he sighs again. He's trying to write about *Stormin' Normans*, one of the Horrible History books. He furrows his brow and tries to focus on the page but he can't do it and his eyes swivel again and he spies a first aid kit on the

kitchen counter. He goes over and brings it back to the table. On opening it he discovers a bandage and wraps it around his leg.

'What are you doing?'

'I'm a crusader doctor. I'm bandaging up a leg I've just cut off.'

URBAN TRACTOR

Sitting at a bus stop on Stoke Newington Church Street I heard a sound both familiar yet strange. In the midst of the normal sounds of the city – police sirens, buses, cars, motorbikes, car alarms, road works – came a low rumbling engine rasp. Then, chugging slowly from Green Lanes, along came a weatherbeaten John Deere tractor, pulling some kind of plough/rake contraption. It carried on towards Albion Road then disappeared into the centre of Stoke Newington.

Is this the fashionable drive of choice for the smart Stoke Newington Pretend Farmers?

(I have thought about this – if I was a Stoke Newington Pretend Farmer I'd drive a battered old blue Fordson.)

A BACON SANDWICH
AND A COFFEE: CAFE VINTAGE

Most people, if they pray, pray for material things
— cars, houses, holidays, cash — or stuff like getting
someone nice-looking to love them. I've always
prayed for one thing (and when I say prayed I mean
hoped really hard with my eyes closed): that a really
good cafe would open up just down the end of my
road. As in George Orwell's essay 'The Moon Under
Water', about a mythical perfect pub, there are
several key points for a good cafe:

Great coffee
Excellent bacon sandwiches
Run by good looking women who are into jazz and
poetry or interesting/funny blokes who like
football and/or experimental electronic music
Quiet/good/no music
Near your house
Have a selection of interesting brown sauces for
the bacon sandwich
Also sell tweed jackets/suits
Have a few old books to read
Working wi-fi
Friends will drop in unexpectedly
Have hats you can wear on sunny days

So imagine my delight when I discovered Cafe
Vintage had opened in the old premises vacated

by Tatran/Slovak Cafe (the Expert Milky Coffee Makers). It's run by two sisters who look like they might have been in a band, they sell tweedy clothes and play jazz at a decent level (how many cafes have you been to where they're arguing about where the Miles Davis CD has gone?). The coffee is great — especially the Americano. You won't be able to walk properly for several hours after the bacon sandwich. The men's clothes are the sort of thing you used to see in your Grandad's wardrobe when you were in his bedroom looking for pipes to nick for WWII fighter pilot games. The women's clothes look like your Gran's Sunday best. And as for hats, they have Sergeant Pepper-era German military band peaked caps, to keep the sun out of your eyes when you're tapping away on a laptop.

THE BOTTLE PEN

The stationer breathed a sigh of relief today when I went in and bought four colour cartridges for my printer.

'Ha — you thought I was just going to ask for one envelope,' I said. He smiled weakly, then quickly and with total stationeresque skill shifted his eyes to a display of pens on the counter. They're recycled. 'Made from bottles,' said the stationer. I'd just been in the library on Blackstock Road, reading an article in *New Scientist* about how the distant future for the earth is the extinction of all life, so buying a recycled pen, while a futile gesture, seemed like the right thing to do. Then the stationer's son (Stationer Jnr) came up to me.

'How are you?' he said.

'Poorer after coming into this shop,' I said. The stationer looked hurt.

'I don't mean poorer spiritually. Just financially.'

The stationer smiled.

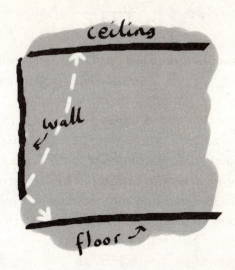

EVERYTHING IS CONNECTED

Every Saturday morning I take the kids to the local swimming baths. We had just got changed and were heading for the training pool when my four-year-old son turned to me and said, 'Dad, everything is connected. Did you know that?'

'In what way?' I asked.

'Well,' he said, 'the floor is connected to the door which is connected to the wall and that's joined to the roof.'

He checked my face to make sure I was suitably impressed then waddled off, looking pleased with himself.

WINTER

(again — but the early bit... if you know what I mean)

Gateway to an other world – around here somewhere

N(ARNIA) 16

The other day, as I tramped happily around in the snow, it occurred to me that in *The Lion, the Witch and the Wardrobe*, C.S. Lewis created Narnia as a metaphor for Clissold Park in Stoke Newington. The gap in the fence on Church Street is the magical entrance to this world, certainly after pub closing time at any rate. Aslan the Lion represents the old bowling green. It's got old lamp posts, deer, an old house.

Did C.S. Lewis spend a lot of time in Stoke Newington and are any of his other books about the area? *A Horse and His Boy* could be about the Lea Valley Riding School. *Prince Caspian* surely refers to that gastropub on Kynaston Road. *The Last Battle* might be a sly comment about the North London anti-bendy bus movement.

Maybe this theory needs a bit more work.

PLANTS I DON'T KNOW
THE NAME OF: LEAVES
TRAPPED IN ICE

The New River appears to be frozen solid, just like it was last year. Caught just below the surface are loads of pale yellow leaves from a something tree, possibly lime, or ash, definitely not hazel or horse chestnut.

HIGHBURY NEW PARK

The gothic back streets of Highbury New Park are
filled with massive villas and even bigger trees.
Gives me the willies. Even on the brightest day, it's
somewhat dark and slightly chilling. I'm never in
the best of spirits here – though I only visit it for the
doctors' surgery.

THE CRAZY MODERNIST BUILDING
AT THE END OF OUR STREET

For years we looked at the crazy modernist building at the end of our street and said 'What a fucking dump!' (It's not exactly Nikolaus Pevsner, I know.) It was either sheltered accommodation or an athletes' village for a joint East German/British Olympic bid in 1972. A few people lived in the crazy modernist building – walking past at night you'd hear crackly garage radio blaring out from an open window, or shouting coming from another window. But nobody ever went in or out.

A few weeks ago the crazy modernist building began gushing water like an incontinent cow. Then a wooden wall was put up around it, which usually means demolition time. I asked a hard-hat bloke what was going up in its place.

'Dunno mate. I only started today.'

So, looks like there will soon be a crazy free-improvised building at the end of our street.

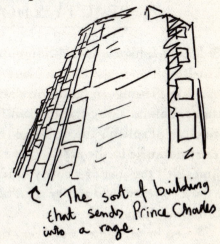

← The sort of building that sends Prince Charles into a rage.

PLANTS I DON'T KNOW THE NAME OF: THE FRUIT TREES BEHIND SLEEPING BEAUTY'S HOUSE

St Mary's Lodge is an old house on the corner of Lordship Road, a still-quiet lane heading north out of Stoke Newington, and Lordship Park, a noisy thoroughfare taking traffic from Highbury to north Hackney. Probably the only surviving grand early Victorian villa in the area, it has fallen on hard times. It's the sort of house you imagine at the end of a dark country road rather than beside a busy road in inner city London.

When my daughter was a very little girl it was still

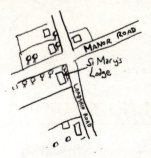

possible to wander around the back of the house into the garden, where there were two large fruit trees. I used to tell her that this was Sleeping Beauty's house and that one day Beauty would awake and the house and garden would come back to life.

'Can we go in, Daddy?' she'd ask.

'Maybe one day, when it comes back to life.' Every day we would pass the house and with great delight she would describe to me what she thought it would have been like in the olden days.

I knew of some people who wanted to buy the house and turn it into an arts centre. But a local school bought it from the council in the early 2000s and then left it to rot for nearly a decade. There was a fire a few years ago and the house was surrounded by boards. A large section of the rear of the house was carted away not long ago. It appears that because they're not allowed to demolish the house the owners are allowing it to be taken apart brick by brick.

We no longer walk to the child-minder's past the house. My daughter doesn't ask about the house any more.

SYLVANIAN FAMILIES TIME

Not that long ago I was in a cafe where the Sylvanian Families marketing team were talking conspiratorially but too loudly about Christmas lines. Look out for a new range of tiny kitchen appliances (possibly for the mice).

More recently I actually visited the shop, for the first time in years, to buy the koala family for a friend. The shop is just round the corner from where we live, yet now it might as well be on the other side of London. We still have the longboat (now languishing in a box in the attic). It's inhabited by the weasel family, along with some WWII soldiers and a plastic Polish footballer figurine.

LOCAL WILDLIFE: THE SEAGULLS

I'm woken from a dream by the sound of birds.
It's a multi-levelled effect, with blackbirds and
starlings in the background, the odd heron (or is a
goose?) flying around aimlessly, but by far the most
dominant noise is seagulls. It could be thousands
of seagulls. Or maybe just four or five – they're
extrovert birds, after all.

I'm being kind – they're fucking annoying and
very loud. I drift in and out of sleep for a while,
washing back to holidays on the pebbled beaches
of South Devon in the early 1970s, the sea pulling
against the stones and the seagulls overhead. I try
to imagine the sound of traffic is like the sea. Then
I remember that film with Rock Hudson (or was it
Cary Grant?) where he's blindfolded and thinks he's
at a party, but it's just the sounds of birds at a lake.

Just around here there were filter beds for Thames
Water which were developed into a housing estate in
the late 1990s. No-one has told the birds that. As far
as they are concerned it is still an unofficial nature
reserve.

THE VIEW FROM THE CHIP SHOP

We all know it's important to be able to see passers-by when you're in a cafe or restaurant. Placement is all. The tall Irish bloke from across the road makes sure he gets the best seat for watching stuff. Whenever I see him in the chippy he is sitting in the same chair, staring out of the window. Eating chips. He is always very friendly, so we have a chat, similar in content to most of our previous conversations.

'You've got a good spot there.'

'It's important to have a good view,' he smiles, leaning back in his chair. 'I've been coming to this chippy since the 80s. It's a great location.'

'Yes, it's a good view, all right. You can see the dry cleaner's across the road.'

'And people like to look in, too,' he laughs.

'If anyone invaded this part of Highbury you'd spot them a mile off from here. It's like a modern version of a castle watchtower. Except with chips.'

He laughs again. 'It has got good *feng shui* all right.'

STICKS

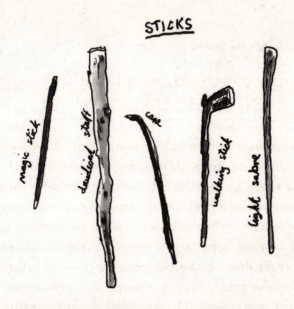

magic stick · druidical staff · cane · walking stick · light sabre

TRADITIONAL CRAFTS

For several years I've been collecting sticks of various lengths, mostly from the local park but some from more rural settings. I've got hazel, ash, beech and various bits that I don't know. My idea was to start making walking sticks/canes at the weekend as a way of getting acquainted with rural crafts but I've hit a snag. The sticks have mostly disappeared, appropriated by my sons for games of Star Wars (they are used as lightsabers), Robin Hood (staffs) and Harry Potter (they are sort-of-broomsticks).

LOCAL WILDLIFE:
NORTH LONDON MUMS

What is it about North London mums? I can't stop thinking about them. They push prams. They smile a lot. They drink coffee. They used to work in the media or publishing. In a way I have more in common with mums than I do with many of the dads around here, in the sense that I don't wear a suit and I don't go anywhere to work. And I like coffee. Although there are more dads around the playground these days, some mornings I am still surrounded by North London mums. So, over the years, my football banter has diminished and my ability to empathise with trying to get the kids to school on time has increased considerably. Naturally I try not to fancy the mums I know but sometimes I can't help it.

I watch them as they stand around in their little groups, cooing over a small child. Then very quickly they all rush off for a coffee and the streets are deserted.

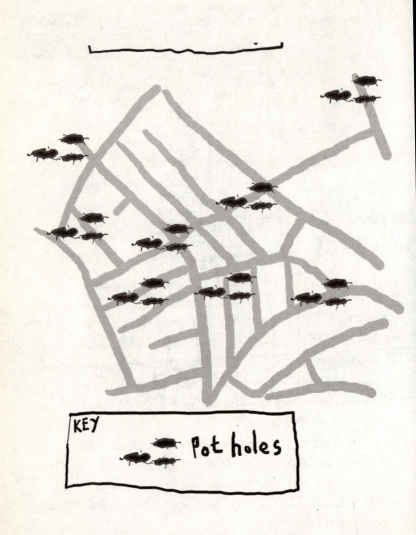

KEY

Pot holes

North London pot holes

MAPPING THE TERRAIN:
POTHOLES

It happened quite suddenly, perhaps due to a
succession of bad winters and also the recession,
but in this part of North London the roads are
crumbling and full of potholes. Some streets have
long crevices like the limestone Burren in the West of
Ireland. Others have circles that fill with water, or a
succession of small dips, with bits of older roads now
showing through.

I walked around a few streets and logged the
incidence of potholes. It made me feel both childlike
and important, like a council road expert or 'road
journalist'. Then I went for a sandwich and stopped
feeling important.

TRADITIONAL CRAFTS: PROCRASTINATING THROUGH WAND-MAKING

I'm up against it with a couple of deadlines, so am doing what any self-respecting freelancer would do: carving a magic wand for one of the kids out of a dead pear bush that's been lying around in the shed for a while. It's very relaxing and, as long as you don't cut one of your fingers off, helps slow down time for a while. Of course I'm creating more problems for myself — once this is in the hands of an ambitious child wizard like our seven-year-old, we'll find that homework has been banned for ever, the kitchen has been turned into a swimming pool, his bedroom is a theme park and I spend all day making candy floss.

RUNNING FOR BUSES

I've always prided myself on my ability to catch
a bus. It doesn't usually matter how far I have to
run, I always make it just in time. But yesterday I
was defeated. At Mornington Crescent, I saw a 29
coming down the road and started a slow jog in
preparation for the big sprint to the bus stop. Maybe
it was because this was a bendy bus that I got it wrong
– but I left the sprint too late. When I got to the bus
stop the doors had closed and the driver ignored my
'palms out' gesture of negotiation.

   As the bus pulled off I suddenly felt old. This
just doesn't happen to me. Then I made a crucial
mistake. 'I'll wait for a 253,' I thought to myself. But
the 253 comes down from Euston along the parallel
road next to the tube. By the time I'd worked this out
I'd been waiting for fifteen minutes. I thought I'd
run down to Camden High Street to the next stop.
But my legs had gone.

NORTH LONDON COMPENDIUM OF LOST THINGS: THE NAME OF THE WOMAN OUT OF HOT GOSSIP

I'm out in the park, on a grey day, under the trees, but I'm not really noticing anything. Instead I'm trying to remember the name of the singer who had that hit with Hot Gossip in 1978. 'I Lost My Heart to a Starship Trooper'. She was The Woman Out Of Hot Gossip. But there's a hole in my memory where her name used to be. I watched them on *Top of the Pops* when I was thirteen, so I know she existed, in fact she ended up marrying Andrew Lloyd Webber. Was it Elaine Page? Arlene Philips? Sheena Easton? Gloria Steinem? Maybe it was Anthea Turner. No, that doesn't feel right. How did this hole get there? Has it been stolen, like that planet in the Jedi Temple's hologram map in *Star Wars II: Attack of the Clones*? Maybe this is why I can never remember the names of trees or plants as well.

How are you supposed to remember stuff without resorting to looking it up? One problem is that the internet is robbing me of the ability to remember names. Somebody asked me recently, 'Who would play you in a film?' and I said, 'Ooh, yeah, I know, er, oh . . . that blond bloke who's a bit beardy. Erm, he was in *State and Main* and also that film about the wife/girlfriend who commits suicide. And he played Truman Capote.' 'You mean Philip Seymour Hoffman?' And I said 'Yes!'

I've been concentrating really hard all day, trying to think of the name of The Woman Out Of Hot Gossip but it still won't come, just this bleached-out area of nothing, with dancers cavorting about all around it. It was just a sequence of thoughts and then it came to a stop with whatever-her-name-is. Why do I want to know anyway? It's a matter of principle. I must get my memory working again. And I refuse to look this up on Google.

Walking in nature is sometimes good for coming up with ideas. Maybe it will be good for accessing damaged memory circuits.

Was it Susan Stranks?

RAIN

It's sheeting down with rain. I'm walking, at a decent
clip, in the direction of Holloway Road, though, of
course, I could go anywhere. There's a slight sadness
– I lost my really good waterproof jacket somewhere
not that long ago. This new one hasn't quite bedded
in yet.

I like walking in the rain. I take it one step at a
time – in the sense that I actually notice my steps.
With the water stinging my face, it feels like a good
day.

Somehow the rain stops you thinking about the
future. I am fully in the present and feeling alive
as I pass the Greggs on Holloway Road then cross
over near the closed-down insurance office. In the
distance I can already see the lollipop lady at the end
of Liverpool Road.

The sound of the rain is calming, like white noise,
blocking out the rumble of traffic and the chatter of
things I have to do. As the rain gets heavier, I feel
like I'm moving forwards – making the future come
to me. And getting really wet thighs because this new
waterproof is just a bit too short.

INTERACTIVE EXERCISES
AND FIELD NOTES

The following pages are part of a training programme designed to make you an urban country diarist of your own area.

NORMAL PERSON   URBAN COUNTRY DIARIST

GET IN THE ZONE

1. Write a haiku* about one of your local shops

_____

_____

_____

*Three-line, seventeen-syllable poem in 5-7-5 format, i.e.:
At the newsagents
'Have you got *The Guardian*?'
'No – it's too left-wing!'

2. What three things did you most like doing when you were ten years old?

_____

_____

_____

(For me it was watching old horror films, drawing on walls and teasing my brothers.)

3. Draw a picture of one of your favourite childhood memories

4. Draw a map of a place you lived or visited as a kid (with places you played or friends' houses)

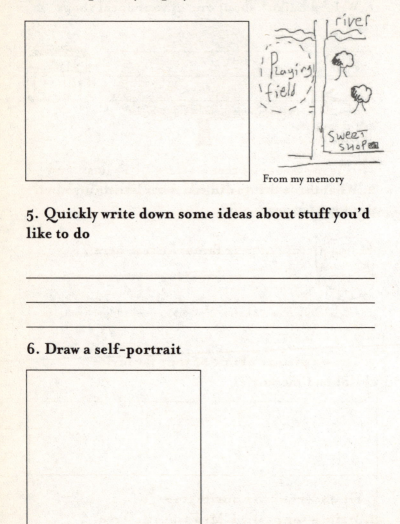

From my memory

5. Quickly write down some ideas about stuff you'd like to do

_____

_____

_____

6. Draw a self-portrait

7. Now go for a walk...

YOUR FAVOURITE TREE

This is my favourite tree – where I like to sit and think about 'stuff' (or think about sitting and thinking).

Draw a picture of your favourite tree here

1. Sit under your favourite tree
2. Write a song called 'My Favourite Tree'
3. Have a picnic under the tree
4. Lean up against your tree and have a kip

NATURE SPOTTING

Are you a sharp-eyed nature detective? Give yourself one point for each of these you spot.

dead bird ☐

empty can of extra-strong lager ☐

Erm... thingy plant ☐

lost teddy ☐

angry dog ☐

angry-looking bloke ☐

(3 pts for bloke and dog together) ☐

Gone *Gone* *Gone* bike with wheels and seat missing ☐

kite up a tree ☐

shopping trolley (not in a supermarket, of course) ☐

? some kind of 'leaf' ☐

HOW TO DRAW... A DOG

1. Draw a circle in pencil

2. Draw another circle

3. Now draw a slightly
cack-handed oval

4. Add some strange
sausage-shaped legs

5. Now fill in the detail
with a pen

6. Erase the guide marks

7. Oh no – I hope his owner
is going to clear that up

8. I don't think the owner is
going to clear that up

HOW TO DRAW...
AN ANGRY-LOOKING BLOKE

1. Draw a circle in pencil

2. Another one... etc

3. More circles, big and little

4. Now fill in the picture with a pen — remember angry eyebrows!

5. Now rub out the pencil marks — and there he is

6. Oh dear, he's seen us — time to get out of here

DRAW PEOPLE...

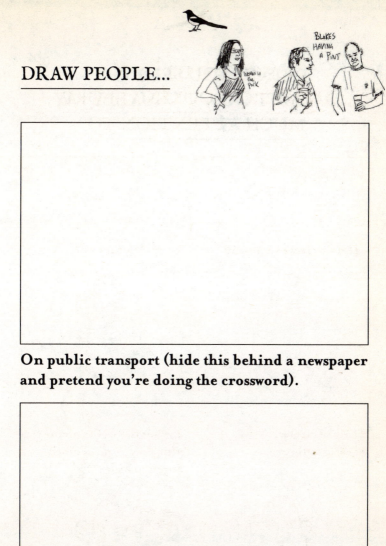

WOMAN in the Park

BLOKES HAVING A PINT

On public transport (hide this behind a newspaper and pretend you're doing the crossword).

In your local park (sit under a tree and watch the joggers and Dog People go past) or in a pub.

THINGS YOU SEE EVERY DAY BUT DON'T USUALLY PAY MUCH ATTENTION TO

...people in shops, cyclists, parents with pushchairs, trees, workmen, old people, houses, benches, cracks in the pavement, flowers in front gardens, dogs...

STOKE NEWINGTONISE THE NEWS

Draw a beard on photos of people in the news, or celebrities. Then cut them out, stick them in here and pretend they are all from Stoke Newington.

CUT HERE

handy beard template

DRAW SOME PLANTS YOU DON'T KNOW THE NAME OF

It's very rewarding to sit and sketch plants and flowers. Having to know what they're called just adds needless stress to the project.

thingy